Olivera Grbić

Serbian Cuisine

Translated from Serbian by: Vladimir D. Janković

ALL TRADITIONAL PLATES

Belgrade, 2014.

Olivera Grbić
SERBIAN CUISINE

Translated from Serbian by
Vladimir D. Janković

Original title
Srpska kuhinja

Editor-in-Chief:
Dijana Dereta

Edited by:
Aleksandar Šurbatović

Artistic and Graphic Design:
Goran Grbić

ISBN 978-86-7346-930-0

Print run:
1500 copies

Belgrade, 2014.

Published / Printed / Marketed by:
DERETA doo
Vladimira Rolovića 94a, 11030, Belgrade
e-mail: office@dereta.rs
Phone / Fax: 381 11 23 99 077; 23 99 078
www.dereta.rs

© Dereta doo

DERETA Bookstores
Knez Mihailova 46, Belgrade; phone: +381 11 30 33 503; 26 27 934
Dostojevskog 7, Banovo Brdo, Belgrade, phone: 381 30 58 707; 35 56 445

CONTENTS

INTRODUCTION

Since ancient times, mores and amenities have played an important role in preserving the identity of a people. Most of the Serbian population in the Middle Ages were *sebri* – farmers with a rich tradition, and all the richness of Serbian cuisine is derived from its geographic, ethnic and cultural diversity, which result from centuries of population mixing. Through the preserved Serbian cuisine recipes, the reader will get to know some ethnic motifs, and only a small part of huge Serbian natural resources. Today we witness many examples of the adjustment of tradition to a completely different, modern way of life. However, the old values and respect for nature have never been entirely suppressed in Serbia.

Cold Appetizers

When it comes to the traditional cold appetizers in Serbian cuisine, the aspic (*pihtiye*) should be certainly mentioned first. This Serbian dish is made from pork legs, head, ears, and other parts that give a good jelly. In some parts of Serbia the smoked meat is added too, so this dish, cut into equal cubes, is simply a must on each slava menue. With aspic, which is prepared mainly during winter, in the time of numerous Serbian slavas, sauerkraut salad and pickles are served, and domestic brandy: strong plum, apricot or quince *rakija*.

NISH STYLE ASPIC

INGREDIENTS:
3,3 lb (1½ kg) of clean porc legs,
meat of leg or ears
1 bunch of greens
1 bay leaf
A few grains of white pepper
1 onion
1 head of garlic
Salt to taste

RECIPE:
Aspic is served as appetizer, and you prepare it this way: take 3.3 pounds (1½ kg) of clean porc legs, meat of leg, and ears (avoid those excessively greasy parts). Wash all thoroughly, put in a larger pot and pour water, until the meat is submerged. Cook over a low heat. When the foam appears on the surface, take the pot off the heat and add a bunch of greens, a bay leaf, a few grains of white pepper, one onion, a head of garlic, and salt, if needed. Cooking should take 4–5 hours, which depends on when the meat softens. When the meat starts falling off the bones, and aspic water becomes sticky, you'll know that the dish is ready. Take off the pot then, and wait until its content settles down. Remove the fat from the surface, then pour the content through a strainer. When strained, separate meat from the bones, chop the larger parts from the leg, and divide it in several deep dishes. Sprinkle with chopped garlic, pour soup over each dish, and then store the plates in a cool place, until the aspic is set.

STERLET ASPIC

INGREDIENTS:
- 2 lb (1 kg) of sterlet
- 1 lb (½ kg) of onions
- ½ lb (¼ kg) of mushrooms
- 8.5 fl oz (1/4 l) of olive oil

RECIPE:

Take 1 kg (2 lb) of sterlet, ½ kg (1 lb) of onions and (¼ kg) ½ pound of fresh mushrooms. It is more difficult to clean sterlet than any other fish; the best way is to scald it in boiling water, and then skin it; you shoud remove its gills and discard them. Chop the onions as finely as you can, salt them and add in a cup (2,5 dl) of olive oil, then fry over a low heat. When the onions are half fried, chop the mushrooms into small pieces, and add them to the onions. While the onions turn to mush, add the chopped fish, and let it simmer for a couple of minutes. Add some cayenne pepper, ground white pepper, and carefuly stir with a scoop. Pour the warm water over fish, until it has submerged, and boil for a half an hour. While boiling, do not stir the fish with a scoop, just shake the pot occasionally. Before removing the pot from heat, add some finely chopped parsley, and allow it to simmer a little bit more. Remove the pot from heat, pour the content in the dishes, and put them in a cool place for the aspic to set.

BEAN ASPIC

INGREDIENTS:
  2 lb (1 kg) of pork feet
  0.9 gal (4 l) of water
  1 onion
  10 grains of pepper
  1 bunch of greens
  2 lb (1 kg) of Tetovo beans

RECIPE:

One kilo (2 lb) of pork feet, washed in several waters, put in a pot and pour 4 liters (0.9 imperial gallon) of cold water. As soon as the water boils, add a garlic head, 10 grains of pepper, some greens, then salt everything, and boil. The soup should be cooked over low heat. When it boils, remove foam from the surface. In a separate pot place some Tetovo beans, boil them, then change the so-called first water, pour the second one, add some onion, and cook until the beans begin to dissolve. Add salt to taste, and divide equally in deep dishes. Pour the aspic soup, previously strained, over each dish. Arrange the meat over the beans, and leave to cool.

HOOPLA (URNEBES) SALAD

INGREDIENTS:
   1 lb (½ kg) of hard cow cheese
   3 hard boiled eggs, 1 onion
   3 tablespoons of ayvar
   2 teaspoons of ground or crushed
   ayenne pepper
   6–7 cloves of garlic
   1 tablespoon of kaymak
   7 fl oz (2 dcl) of oil

RECIPE:
Take ½ kg (1 lb) of hard cow cheese and strain it. Using a fork, add 3 strained hard boiled eggs, some finely chopped onion, 3 tablespoons of ayvar, 2 teaspoons of ground or crushed cayenne pepper, 6–7 cloves of garlic, one tablespoon of kaymak, 2 dl (7 fl oz) of oil, and then thoroughly whisk all the ingredients.

PICKLED PEPPERS STUFFED WITH CHEESE AND KAYMAK

INGREDIENTS:
    2 lb (1 kg) of green or yellow peppers
    1 lb (½ kg) of cow cheese
    3–4 tablespoons of sour cream
    3–4 tablespoons of kaymak
    2–3 pt (1–1.5 l) of salted milk

RECIPE:
Take 1 kg (2 lb) of yellow or green peppers, and clean the seeds and stems. Using a fork, mash in a bowl ½ kg (1 lb) of cow cheese, 3–4 tablespoons of sour cream and the same amount of kaymak, so the mixture is creamy. Stuff the peppers with this mixture, and arrange in the jars. Pour some salted milk over the peppers in the jars, and let them sit for 2 days. Every 2 days separate waste water from milk in the jars and pour new milk, until it acquires an unique fragrance which is a sign that peppers are ready for appetizer use.

Soups
and Broths

In Serbia they say: „I haven't eaten if I haven't used a spoon!" No lunch, whether ordinary or formal, can be imagined without a soup or a broth. Many different kinds of soups and broths are prepared in Serbia, but the most common are Serbian young beef broth, chiken broth, lamb broth, as well as beef soup and chicken soup.

Broths are rich with meat and vegetables, and often very spicy.

Soups are clear, and served with noodles or dumplings. However, there is a soup that combines all the good qualities: Shumadian (*šumadijska, from Šumadija*), or Peasant soup. Chicken cut into sticks, carrot, parsnip, celery and one onion are cooked, with ground pepper and finely chopped parsley added.

DOCK BROTH

INGREDIENTS:
   2 lb (1 kg) of veal or beef bones
   1 bunch of greens
   1 onion
   3.5 oz (100 g) of bacon
   1 clove of garlic
   A few peppercorns

RECIPE:

Wash and boil 1 kg (2 lb) of veal or beef bones. Then wash 1 kg (2 lb) of dock leaves, chop them into strips, season with salt, and let stand until they release a green juice. In a sepa-rarate pan place a tablespoon of fat, add a tablespoon of flour and, when browned flour is ready, pour the previously strained dock leaves on it, and add the soup in which the bones have been boiled.

Take then 100 g (3.5 oz) of bacon, dice it, fry to a golden brown and add to soup. The bacon will make this broth taste even better. Season the broth, add some peppercorns, and let it simmer with the browned flour and bacon for at least half an hour. In a large tureen put one egg yolk, 3–4 tablespoons of sour cream and some sour milk, and slowly pour the broth over it. Thus seasoned, serve the broth.

SOUR LAMB SOUP

INGREDIENTS:

1 lb (½ kg) of lamb meat
3.5 pts (2 l) of water
1 bunch of greens, parsley
A few grains of black pepper
1 tablespoon of fat
2 tablespoons of flour
A pinch of cayenne pepper
1 egg yolk, 7 fl oz (2 dcl) of sour milk
Vinegar or lemon juice to taste

RECIPE:

For 4 people, take half a kilo (1 lb) of lamb meat. Cut the meat into pieces, wash it, put in a small pot, and pour 2 liters (3.5 pints) of cold water. When the meat starts to boil, add some greens, a little parsley, one onion and a few grains of black pepper. The soup should not be cooked on high heat. After about 2 hours, make a browned flour: in a small pan put a table-spoon of fat and, when heated, add 2 tablespoons of flour, and let it fry until it is yellow. Then add a pinch of cayenne pepper, put the browned flour in it, and leave to cook for another half hour. Strain, and then season the dish like this: in a large tureen put one egg yolk, 2 dl (7 fl oz) of sour milk and, while stirring constantly, slowly pour the hot soup over. Add some vinegar or lemon juice to taste.

LEEK AND CHICKEN BROTH

INGREDIENTS:
   3 pts (1.5 l) of water
   1 lb (½ kg) of chicken meat
   4 average sized leeks
   3–4 potatoes
   2 egg yolks
   2 tablespoons of sour cream
   1 teaspoon of butter

RECIPE:
Put the chicken meat in a pot with cold water, and cook on low heat. In the meantime, clean 4 average sized leeks from green leaves, and then cut the white parts to length, in 4 pieces. Boil them together with 3–4 potatoes, drain and mash. Pour the chicken broth over it, season with salt and pepper, and leave to boil. You should not brown the flour for this broth, but, when it's finished, add a piece of butter and two egg yolks beaten with a little sour cream. Than you can serve the dish.

POTATO BROTH

INGREDIENTS:

    2 lb (1 kg) of potatoes
    1 tablespoon of fat
    ½ tablespoon of flour
    ½ teaspoon of cayenne pepper
    1 bell pepper
    1 egg yolk
    3 tablespoons of sour cream
    2 tablespoons of lemon juice

RECIPE:

Take 1 kg (2 lb) of potatoes, peel them, wash and dice. Put a tablespoon of fat or oil and half a spoon of flour in a pot. Add a little cayenne pepper, and put the potatoes on the browned flour, stir, and then pour the bone soup over it. Add salt, finely chopped parsley leaves, one bell pepper, and cook together. In a large tureen put an egg yolk, 3 tablespoons of sour cream and 2 tablespoons of vinegar or lemon juice. Stir well, slowly baste with the broth, and serve.

PEA BROTH

INGREDIENTS:
½ lb (250 g) of young peas
½ onion
1 tablespoon of fat
1 tablespoon of flour, 1 egg yolk
2 tablespoons of sour cream
1 teaspoon of lemon juice
Bone soup
Dill leaves
Salt

RECIPE:
Put a tablespoon of fat in a pan and, when well heated, add a half of a finely cut onion. When onion is fried, add a ¼ kg (½ pound) of young peas, and fry until they soften. Add a tablespoon of flour to the peas, fry together, pour the bone soup over, salt to taste, put a few dill leaves and continue cooking. At the end, season with an egg yolk, some sour cream and the lemon juice.

BEAN BROTH

INGREDIENTS:
    1 lb (½ kg) of beans
    ½ lb (¼ kg) of dried meat
    1 onion
    1 bell onion
    1 tablespoon of flour
    1 tablespoon of fat
    A pinch of cayenne pepper
    Salt

RECIPE:

Take ½ kg (1 lb) of beans, put them in a pot, pour cold water and let it cook. Pour off the first water, and replace it with another, hot water. Add onion, salt, one bell pepper, and cook all together until beans are quite soft. Mash the cooked beans with a fork. Put a tablespoon of fat in a pot and, when heated, add a tablespoon of flour. When the flour is well fried, sprinkle some cayenne pepper on it, and then add those mashed beans. Dilute with water in which you previously cooked ¼ kg (½ lb) of dried meat. Cut the dried meat into small pieces, add it to the broth, and serve.

BEEF SOUP

INGREDIENTS:
  2 lb (1 kg) of beef
  1 bunch of greens
  1 onion
  1 clove of garlic
  Noodles, flakes or semolina dumplings
  Salt, Pepper

RECIPE:
Wash 1 kg (2 lb) of beef from the breast, put it in the pot, and pour cold water over. Add some greens, one onion, a slice of cabbage, one clove of garlic. Season the soup with salt, and add a few black peppercorns. Allow to boil, but slowly, because the desired taste depends on simmering. As soon as it boils, remove the foam from the surface, and leave to simmer until the meat is cooked. Strain the soup, and cook up the noodles, flakes or semolina dumplings, depending on your preferences.

DRIED MEAT SOUP

INGREDIENTS:
¼ lb (½ kg) of dried meat
1 onion, 1 bunch of greens
2–3 tablespoons of strained tomatoes
2 cloves of garlic
3.5 fl oz (1 dcl) of sour cream
1 tablespoon of flour, a pinch of cayenne
  pepper, a few drops of vinegar
1 egg yolk, 1 tablespoon of sour cream

RECIPE:
Take ½ kg (¼ lb) of dried meat, washed in 2–3 warm waters, put it in a pot, pour cold water and cook until the meat is half soft. Add one onion and a bunch of greens. When the soup is ready, remove the meat, and add 2–3 tablespoons of strained tomatoes, as well as 2 cloves of garlic. Let the soup boil a little, then slowly pour the spice which you prepare like this: in 1 dl (3.5 fl oz) of sour cream mix a teaspoonful of flour, a pinch of cayenne pepper and some vinegar. Put an egg yolk and sour cream in a large tureen, and pour the soup over, little by little.

VEAL BROTH

INGREDIENTS:
  2 lb (1 kg) of veal
  3.5 pts (2 l) of water
  1 bunch of greens
  1 bell pepper, 1 tomato, 1 onion
  1 tablespoon of fat, 1 tablespoon of flour
  A pinch of cayenne pepper
  2 egg yolks, 7 fl oz (2 dcl) of sour milk
  Salt and pepper

RECIPE:
Take 1 kg (2 lb) of veal, cut it into pieces, put in a pot, pour over 2 litres (3.5 pints) of cold water, and let it cook. Add some greens, one tomato, one bell pepper, one onion, salt and pepper. The browned flour you prepare this way: heat a tablespoon of fat in a pan, and then add a tablespoon of flour; fry the flour a little, and then add a pinch of cayenne pepper. Pour a cup of cold water so the flour is not lumpy. Put the browned flour in the pot with meat, and let the broth simmer until the meat softens. Take the meat out, and strain the broth. In a large tureen put 2 egg yolks and 2 dl (7 fl oz) of sour milk, and stir. Slowly pour the strained broth over the seasoning mix, add vinegar to taste, and serve.

FISH SOUP

INGREDIENTS:
    4.4 lb (2 kg) of various small fish
    7 oz (200 g) of onions
    1 bunch of parsley
    1–2 stalks of celery
    1 bay leaf
    1 teaspoon of white pepper
    1 fresh pepper, 2 egg yolks
    Vinegar,
    Salt

RECIPE:
Take 2 kg (4.4 lb) of various small fish: little carp, pike, white fish. Clean them and slice crosswise, place them into the pan and cover with chopped onions. Add some parsley, one or two stalks of celery, a bay leaf, one teaspoon of white peppercorn and one pepper. Pour cold water and boil at a low heat. After a while, turn up the heat and let it boil for half an hour. In a large tureen, in which you will serve the soup, put 2 egg yolks and add vinegar to taste, a spoonful of cold soup, and then slowly pour the hot soup from the pot.

Hot Appetizers

In the past, hot appetizers in the Serbian cuisine mainly consisted of dairy products, which could be found in abundance, as well as of wheat and corn, and, a little less, meat and vegetables. Of the cereals that are largely used today, the Serbs made *cicvara, kačamak, proja,* and many different kinds of pies with stretched crusts, dock leaves and cheese or sauerkraut, as well as many other dishes that still can be tasted in all parts of modern Serbia.

FRITTERS

INGREDIENTS:
    4 eggs
    24 tablespoons of flour
    7 fl oz (2 dcl) of sour milk
    1 teaspoon of baking powder
    Salt

RECIPE:
Put 4 eggs, 24 tablespoons of flour, 2 dcl (7 fl oz) of sour milk, a sachet of baking powder and some salt in a large bowl. Knead it all well, remove the dough with a tablespoon, and put in the heated oil. The fried fritters you can serve sweet, by rolling them in icing sugar, or salty, with kaymak and cheese.

TSITSVARA

INGREDIENTS:
   1 pint (½ l) sour cream
   2 tablespoons of white flour
   Salt

RECIPE:

In a pint (½ liter) of sour cream mix 2 tablespoons of white flour. Put the mixture in a saucepan and stir over a heat until it becomes a thick mass, and the fat from it reaches the surface. Then drain and serve while warm.

CORNBREAD

INGREDIENTS:
- ½ lb (¼ kg) of kaymak
- ½ lb (¼ kg) of cheese
- ½ lb (¼ kg) of corn flour
- 8.5 fl oz (¼ l) of milk
- 4 eggs
- 1 tablespoon of lard

RECIPE:
It takes a ¼ kg (½ lb) of kaymak, ¼ kg (½ lb) of cheese, one tablespoon of lard, ¼ kg (½ lb) of corn flour, ¼ liter (8.5 fl oz) of milk and 4 eggs. First knead the kaymak, cheese, egg yolks, a tablespoon of lard, and milk, then add the flour and previously beaten egg whites, so the dough gets pretty sloppy. Put the dough in the greased casserole, and bake with high heat until it is golden brown.

POLENTA WITH CHEESE

Ingredients:
1 pint (½ liter) of water
1 lb (½ kg) of cornmeal
½ lb (¼ kg) of cheese
½ lb (¼ kg) of kaymak
1 tablespoon of lard
A pinch of cayenne pepper

Recipe:
In a pint (½ liter) of boiling salted water slowly pour ½ kg (1 lb) of cornmeal, and stir constantly to prevent formation of lumps. When the flour is well cooked, reduce heat and keep on stirring. When cooked, you serve polenta like this: take a bowl, pour the first layer of polenta, then cheese and kaymak above it, then another polenta layer, and so on, until you reach the top of the bowl. For this amount of polenta, you need ¼ kg (½ lb) of cheese and ¼ kg (½ lb) of kaymak. In warm bowls pour about a tablespoon of heated fat, with a bit of cayenne pepper, and serve.

MANTLES

INGREDIENTS:
  1 ½ lb (700 g) of flour
  1 teaspoon of salt
  13.5 fl oz (400 ml) of water
  1.4 oz (40 g) of butter
  1 onion
  13.5 oz (400 g) of ground beef
  3 tablespoons of butter
  Salt and pepper

RECIPE:
In a large bowl mix together 700 g (1½ lb) of flour, a teaspoon of salt, 400 ml (13.5 fl oz) of water, and stir until dough softens. Leave it to rest for half an hour. Take another vessel and heat 40 g (1.4 oz) of butter, and fry one finely chopped onion. Add then 400 g (13.5 oz) of ground beef, some salt and pepper, and leave over heat until the water evaporates. Remove from heat and leave to cool. Knead the dough, divide it into 8 little balls, brush with melted butter and let stand for another 20 minutes. Flatten each one with a rolling pin, and then stretch the dough with your hands so the piecrusts (layers of dough) are thin. Coat each piecrust with butter and arrange on top of another one. When this is done, cut the arranged piecrusts in 15 equal squares and fill each one evenly with chilled meat. Fold filled squares by joining diagonal corners, and put them in a baking pan coated with butter. When the pan is filled, brush the mantles with butter and bake with high heat for about half an hour.

POTATO DOUGHNUT

INGREDIENTS:
  9 oz (280 g) of potatoes
  9 oz (280 g) of flour
  2.25 oz (70 g) of fat
  1 oz (20 g) of yeast
  3 egg yolks
  Sour cream, boiled ham, grated
  cow cheese, and salt as needed

RECIPE:

Take 280 g (9 oz) of boiled and peeled potatoes, mash them, and then add the same amount (9 oz) of flour, 70 g (2.25 oz) of fat, a little salt, 3 egg yolks and 20 g (1 oz) of yeast stirred in a little milk. Add sour cream to the dough, so it is neither too soft nor too hard. Knead it all well, and then make small doughnuts, which you will stuff with finely sliced ham, following these instructions: flatten the doughnuts with a rolling pin, cut the dough using a round mold, and place the ham stuffing on each of them. Cover the stuffing with unfilled dough loaf, and take out the pieces of dough out as muffins. Let them swell, and then fry in deep, hot oil, so they brown first on one side, then on another. When doughnuts are baked and hot, sprinkle them with grated cheese, arrange on a larger plate, and serve.

MEAT PIE

INGREDIENTS:
  2 lb (1 kg) of flour
  1 tablespoon of oil
  3 tablespoons of fat
  1 onion
  2 lb (1 kg) of ground veal
  1 egg
  Pepper and salt as needed

RECIPE:
Take 1kg (2 lb) of flour, salt it, add one tablespoon of oil, then add water and knead until the dough begins to pull away from the your hands. When the dough is prepared, divide it into 3 parts, roll them with a rolling pin, anoint with melted fat, cover using a clean tablecloth, and let stand for at least 15 minutes. Roll the piecrusts (layers of dough) until they become thin, and leave them to dry. In the meanwhile, put a tablespoon of fat in the pan, add one chopped onion and, when fried, add 1 kg (2 lb) of ground veal and fry well. Remove from heat, and add pepper, salt and an egg. Dried piecrusts sprinkle with hot fat, fold all four sides toward the center, adjust the piecrust size to the dimensions of the casserole, and then place the first folded crust to the bottom of the vessel. Repeat the same with another piecrust. Put some filling, spread it evenly, and brush with hot grease. Take then the other stretched piecrust, spread the meat filling over it, and then put the last piecrust, as the final layer, over it. Bake the pie, sprinkle it with cold water and cover with a clean tablecloth so it is soft, but not breakable. Cut it into cubes, and serve.

GIBANITZA

INGREDIENTS:
 2 lb (1 kg) of flour
 1 tablespoon of butter
 2 tablespoons of fat
 1 lb (½ kg) of cheese
 1 lb (½ kg) of kaymak
 10 eggs
 Milk and salt as needed

RECIPE:
One kilo (2 lb) of flour knead in salted water, then add a piece of butter or a tablespoon of fat. Keep on kneading until the dough begins to pull away from your hands. This amount of flour should be enough to make 24 small dough loaves; flatten each of them using a rolling pin, spread with hot grease, and then take two by two, roll them thin, and bake on a stove. Baked piecrusts, still warm, wrap in a tablecloth so they do not get cold and harder to break. Follow these steps to prepare the filling: take ½ kg (¼ lb) of cheese, ½ kg (1 lb) of kaymak and 10 egg yolks, and beat all well. Whisk the egg whites firm, mix them with cheese and kaymak, then add a little milk and fat, so the mass is thinner. On a coated baking pan place crust by crust dipped in the filling, until you have used them all. Arranged gibanitza you can pierce with a fork, then sprinkle with milk and brush with some more fat. Put it into the oven, and bake until golden brown.

SPINACH PIE

INGREDIENTS:
    2 lb (1 kg) of flour
    1 tablespoon of butter
    1 lb (½ kg) of spinach
    ½ lb (¼ kg) of kaymak
    1 lb (½ kg) of cheese
    1 tablespoon of bread crumbs
    1 tablespoon of flour, 4 eggs
    Salt as needed

RECIPE:
Knead one kilogram (2 lb) of flour with salted water, and then add a piece of butter or a tablespoon of fat. Keep on kneeding it until the dough begins to pull away from your hands. Divide dough into small loaves, roll each one out into a thin piecrust, and leave to dry. In the meantime, make the filling. Clean ½ kg (¼ lb) of spinach, wash in several waters, cut it in thin strips, add some salt, and leave to sit for a while. Then drain the spinach with your hands, and add ¼ kg (½ lb) of kaymak, ½ kg (1 lb) of cheese, a little bread crumbs and flour, and 4 whole eggs. Mix it all well. Brush the dried piecrust with fat, fold it on all four sides, so it fits the pan, then put it in a coated baking pan, and brush with some more fat. Repeat the procedure with another piecrust, and then pour the stuffing over both of them. Spread the stuffing evenly, brush with some more fat, and cover it with another two piecrusts, dried and folded the same way.

SCRAMBLED EGGS WITH CHEESE & ROASTED PEPPERS

INGREDIENTS:
- 5 bell peppers
- ½ lb (¼ kg) of kaymak
- 1 tablespoon of butter
- 1 tablespoon of milk
- 4 eggs
- 1 lb (½ kg) of sheep chese
- Salt as needed

RECIPE:
Take bell peppers, grill them, sprinkle with cold water to make peeling easier, cover them with a clean towel, and peel later. When peeled, put them in a colander to drain. Remove seeds and stems, and cut the peppers into strips. Take ¼ kg (½ lb) of kaymak, 100 g (3 oz) of butter, some sweetened milk and chopped peppers, mix it all, and fry. When the dish is half fried, add 4 whole eggs, 1 lb (½ kg) of mashed sheep cheese, and fry it some more. Serve while warm.

SCRAMBLED EGGS WITH CRACKLINGS

INGREDIENTS:
  1 tablespoon of fat
  2–3 onions
  2 tablespoons of cracklings
  2 pickled bell peppers
  2–3 eggs
  Salt and pepper as needed

RECIPE:

In a small amount of fat fry 2–3 finely chopped onions. Add a handful of cracklings, and continue frying. After a little while, pour some water, so the cracklings soften, and stir occasionally until the water evaporates. Cut 2 sour pickled peppers, fry them with onions and cracklings, then break 2–3 eggs in it, salt to taste, season with pepper, and fry it just a little more.

SAUERKRAUT PIE

INGREDIENTS:
   2 lb (1kg) of sauerkraut
   ¼ lb (½ lb) of piecrust
   2 onions
   Cayenne pepper and black
   pepper as needed

RECIPE:
Take 1 kg (2 lb) of sauerkraut, wash it, drain well and chop. Then chop two onions, fry them, add the cabbage, and keep on frying until water evaporates. Add some cayenne pepper and pepper to taste. Arrange thin layers of dough, previously sprinkled with oil, fill with cabbage, and roll in. For this amount of sauerkraut, you shall need no more than ½ kg (1 lb) of piecrust. Arrange filled crusts in a greased baking pan, and bake with high heat until golden brown.

POTATOES WITH CHEESE

Ingredients:
2 lb (1 kg) of potatoes
1 lb (½ kg) of cow cheese
½ lb (¼ kg) of bacon

Recipe:
To prepare this dish you need 1 kg (2 lb) of potatoes, ½ kg (1 lb) of cow cheese and ¼ kg (½ lb) of bacon. Wash the potatoes, put them in a pot, and boil. When boiled, peel them and cut into thin slices. Take a fireproof pan, coat it with slices of bacon, cover them with potatoes, and sprinkle cheese over them. Then comes another layer of potatoes, which you will cover with slices of bacon. Bake until the bacon is golden brown. Serve in the same casserole in which it was made, as an appetizer.

CHEESE STUFFED PEPPERS

INGREDIENTS:
    20 bell peppers
    1 lb (½ kg) of sheep cheese
    6 eggs
    3 tablespoons of fat

RECIPE:
Take 20 bell peppers, seed them, wash and leave to drain. In the meantime, put ½ kg (1 lb) of fresh sheep cheese, and mash it using a fork. Add 6 whole eggs, and mix everything together well. Use this stuffing to fill the cleaned peppers. Place 3 tablespoons of fat in a pan, let it heat up, and then put the peppers in. Rotate them while frying, so they get evenly golden brown. Serve them hot, as an appetizer.

BREADED FRIED PEPPERS

INGREDIENTS:
  2 lb (1 kg) of peppers
  2 tablespoons of fat
  5 eggs
  Bread crumbs as needed

RECIPE:
Take some fleshy bell peppers, or long peppers, and grill them, peel and leave in colander to drain. Put 2 tablespoons of fat in a pan, and let it warm up. Beat 5 whole eggs. Take each pepper and, holding its stem, dip it first into the egg batter and then in bread crumbs, before you fry it in hot fat. Serve them warm.

CORN FLOUR PANCAKE

INGREDIENTS:
  4 oz (125 g) of corn flour
  8 0z (250 g) of wheat flour
  2 tablespoons of vinegar
  7 fl oz (2 dcl) of milk
  3–4 eggs

RECIPE:
Mix 125 g (4 oz) of corn flour with a ¼ kg (8 oz) of wheat flour, pour the mixture in a vessel and make a recess in the middle. Add salt, oil and 2 tablespoons of vinegar, pour 2 dl (7 fl oz) of milk, and knead it all together. Milk should be added gradually. Separately, beat 3–4 eggs and add them, gradually, while continuously kneading the dough. Let the dough rest for some time. It is recommended that you make the dough in the morning, and bake it before lunch. Grease the pan thoroughly, and cook the pancakes as you would any other pancakes. You can sprinkle them with grated cheese, or fill them with jam, depending on your preferences.

UZICE STYLE PUFF PASTRIES

INGREDIENTS:
    1 lb (½ kg) of sausage
    1 tablespoon of fat
    2 onions
    A pinch of parsley
    Puff pastry as needed

RECIPE:
For this pastry you can use sausages filled with meat and liverwurst, if stuffed into the small intestine. Cook the sausages in fat, so they soften, and then let them cool. Remove the sausage tube, and cut the sausage into pieces 15–18 cm (6–7 in) long. Separately, fry 2 finely cut onions, and add a little chopped parsley. Each piece of sausage roll in toasted onion and parsley, place the pieces on puff pastry cut in squares, and fold them so the bottom side is longer than the upper one. Arrange puff pastries in a baking pan, put them into the oven, and bake with high heat until pale yellow.

LARD MUFFINS

Ingredients:
   ½ lb (¼ kg) of lard
   1 lb (½ kg) of flour
   1 oz (20 g) of yeast
   4 eggs
   10 fl oz (3 dcl) of sour cream
   Salt as needed

Recipe:

Take ¼ kg (½ lb) of lard, wash it, clean of blood vessels and grind in a meat mincer. Add ½ kg (1 lb) of flour and 20 g (1 oz) of yeast soaked in a small amout of milk, as well as 4 egg yolks, 3 dl (10 fl oz) of sour cream and salt to taste. Knead the dough and make a piecrust thick as a thumb. Remove muffins using a smaller mold, and brush them with a beaten egg yolk. Arrange them in a baking pan, and leave to rise naturally. Bake them with moderate heat, and serve hot.

Meatless Dishes

Serbian cuisine is very tasty, spicy and irresistibly appetite-increasing. Various types of baked goods, dairy products like cheese and cream, vegetables and spices are used in large quantities, so the choice of meatless dishes is quite satisfactory.

However, more and more Serbs are returning to their roots and, doing so, renew the old custom of fasting.

Meatless meals are not included in the group of vegetarian and macrobiotic dishes; no, these are the dishes that old Serbs prepared during fasting days and weeks. In the preparation of these dishes, no animal fat and meat, eggs, milk and dairy products are used.

Here we should stress what the Orthodox Church emphasizes: fasting is not just giving up fatty foods. To fast means to purify oneself from all indecent and unworthy thoughts, ugly words and everything that the Christian religion deems sinful.

LENTILS WITH RICE

Ingredients:
    2–3 fresh (spring) onions
    3 cloves of garlic, 2 carrots
    7.5 oz (220 g) of mushrooms
    7.5 oz (220 g) of lentils
    7.5 oz (220 g) of rice
    1.75 pt (1 l) of vegetable soup
    7.5 oz (220 g) of kale,
    5 fl oz (150 ml) of yogurt
    Salt, cumin and sesame seeds as needed

Recipe:
Heat a little oil in a pan, and add 2–3 finely chopped fresh onion, 3 cloves of garlic, 2 carrots and 220 g (7.5 oz) of mushrooms. After a while, stir in 220 g (7.5 oz) of rice and the same amount of lentils. Add salt, cumin, ginger and 1 liter (2 pt) of vegetable soup, and let boil. Reduce the heat, cover the pot and let it simmer for another 15 minutes, stirring occasionally. Add 220 g (7.5 oz) of chopped kale, and continue cooking until it softens. Finally, pour 150 ml (5 fl oz) of yogurt over the top, and sprinkle with a pinch of sesame seeds.

BACHELOR STEW

INGREDIENTS:
  1.7 oz (50 g) of fat
  1 lb (½ kg) of onions
  1 lb (½ kg) of fresh tomatoes
  2–3 fresh peppers
  A pinch of cayenne pepper
  Salt to taste

RECIPE:
Cut onions into slices, place them in the heated fat, and let them fry briefly. Take fresh peppers, slice them into rings, and mix with the onions. After 2–3 minutes add a pound of sliced tomatoes, and stir constantly. When the water evaporates, add a little cayenne pepper, stir, and serve while warm

BAKED BEANS

INGREDIENTS:
- 1 lb (½ kg) of Tetovo beans
- 4.5–5 lb (2–2.5 kg) of onions
- 4–5 bay leaves
- 1 teaspoon of cayenne pepper
- Salt and oil as needed

RECIPE:

Cook ½ kg (1 lb) of Tetovo beans. Throw the first water off, then pour the fresh water, and add 4–5 finely chopped onions. When the bean is thoroughly cooked and softened, drain it. In another pan with heated oil place 2 kg (4.4 lb) of onions cut in slices. When fried, add cayenne pepper and remove from heat. Prepare a deep vessel which you will put in the oven, and then arrange the ingredients: first goes a layer of potatoes, then a layer of fried onions. Pour some oil over the onions (you should not economize with oil while making this dish), and then repeat the procedure until the dish is full, while ensuring that the beans are not at the top. Thus prepared beans put into the oven to simmer for half an hour. Baked beans (Prebranatz) can be served either warm or cold.

DRY RED PEPPERS STUFFED WITH BEANS

INGREDIENTS:
- 1 lb (½ kg) of beans
- 15–20 dry peppers
- 2 onions
- 1 cup of rice
- Cayenne
- Boiled tomatoes as needed
- Pepper
- Salt

RECIPE:
Put ½ kg (1 lb) of beans in a pot to cook. Throw the first water off, pour fresh water, and continue cooking. In the meantime, put the dried peppers in boiling water for 10 minutes to soften, while frying 2 finely chopped onions in another vessel. Drain the cooked beans, pour them over the onions, add a cup of rice, salt to taste, and season with a little cayenne pepper and black pepper. For richer flavor you can add a handful of ground walnuts. Use this mixture to stuff peppers, then arrange them in a casserole, pour water until they are submerged, add some boiled tomatoes, and place over heat. When water boils, reduce the heat, and let it simmer at a low temperature.

MEATLESS SARMAS WITH FRESH CABBAGE

INGREDIENTS:
- 1 onion, 4 carrots
- 2 potatoes
- 1 celery root
- 2 yellow squashes
- 1 soup cube
- 7 oz (200 g) of rice
- 2–3 concentrated tomato juice
- 2 tablespoons of cumin

RECIPE:

Grate 4 carrots, 2 bigger potatoes, one smaller celery root, chop one onion, and place all in heated oil. Cook vegetables for about 10 minutes, occasionally adding water. Then add 2 grated yellow squashes, some basil, rosemary, a soup cube, salt and pepper. Pour in more water, and leave vegetables to simmer over a low heat. Add 200 g (7 oz) of rice and 2–3 tablespoons of concetrated tomato juice, then remove from heat and allow to cool. In the meanwhile, put 2 tablespoons of cumin in another vessel, pour some water over it, and place on the heat to boil. Clean cabbage heads and, when the water warms up, put them into it. Scald the cabbage, remove leaves (one at a time), and let them drain. Put the leaves on a flat surface and cover them with a plate, so they flatten out. How to stuff cabbage leaves: the bigger ones cut in half and remove hard vein, while the smaller ones prepare by thinning the vein. Put some stuffing on a leaf, fold one side and roll it, then take the sarma in your hand, stuff the unfolded side, and roll it too. Arrange sarmas in a coated baking pan, brush with oil and bake on high heat until golden brown.

STEWED SAUERKRAUT

INGREDIENTS:
  4.4 lb (2 kg) of sauerkraut
  2–3 onions
  A pinch of cayenne pepper
  1 cup of rice
  1–2 bay leaves
  Grains of black pepper as needed

RECIPE:
Chop the cabbage head of 2 kg (4.4 lb) into strips, wash and thoroughly drain. Heat some oil in a pan. Cut 2–3 small onions, put them in the oil and fry. Mix the cabbage with fried onion, and cook at a lower heat, occasionally adding water or vegetable soup, until the cabbage softens. Then add a pinch of cayenne pepper, a little black pepper, one or two laurel leaves, and one cup of rice. If necessary, add some water too, and then put the dish in the oven to brown.

NEW POTATOES WITH KAYMAK

Ingredients:
2 lb (1 kg) of new potatoes
1 tablespoon of margarine
A pinch of parsley
4 oz (125 g) of kaymak

Recipe:
Clean 1 kg (2 lb) of new (young) potatoes, cut them into slices, season with salt, and leave to stand for half an hour. Put a little butter in a pan, add potatoes and fry until golden brown. Season the potatoes with finely chopped parsley, pour over 125 g (4 oz) of melted kaymak, then let simmer for another 10 minutes. You can serve it with boiled or roasted meat.

GREEN BEANS WITH MILK AND KAYMAK

Ingredients:
    2 lb (1 kg) of green beans
    4 spring onions
    3 carrots
    3–4 cloves of garlic
    1 pt (½ l) of milk
    1 tablespoon of parsley
    2 eggs, 9 oz (250 g) of kaymak
    Salt as needed

Recipe:
Wash and chop 1 kg (2 lb) of green beans. Finely chop 4 spring onions, and fry them in heated oil. Add 3 sliced carrots, 3–4 chopped cloves of garlic, salt and ½ liter (1 pt) of milk, and let fry for half an hour. Then add a tablespoon of chopped parsley, and pour it all in a fireproof casserole coated with margarine. Beat 2 eggs with 250 g (9 oz) of kaymak and 100 ml (3.5 fl oz) of milk, pour the mixture over the grean beans, and bake at a higher temperature.

STUFFED POTATOES

INGREDIENTS:
  2 lb (1 kg) of potatoes
  1 onion
  1–2 cloves of garlic
  3 tablespoons of semolina
  7 fl oz (200 ml) of vegetable soup
  2 egg yolks
  3.5 oz (100 g) of kashkaval cheese
  Salt and pepper to taste

RECIPE:
Wash 1 kg (2 lb) of potatoes and cook them with skins on. Do not overdo them; peel the potatoes while undercooked, then take a spoon and hollow out the center of each one. Chop one onion and 1–2 cloves of garlic, and fry them in heated oil. Add 3 tablespoons of semolina, pour 200 ml (7 fl oz) of vegetable soup, and cook for a couple of minutes while stirring. Remove from heat and add salt, pepper, 2 egg yolks, the potato centers and 100 g (3.5 oz) of grated cheese. Fill the potatoes with this stuffing, arrange them in a baking pan, and bake for 15 minutes. Baked stuffed potatoes serve with cheese, kaymak or salad.

Meat Dishes

ℏistorians say that, in the days of old, only the rich Serbians were those who ate wheat bread, while the poor ones had to satisfy themselves with the oats or rye bread. Milk, dairy products and vegetables were the most common foods. As for meat, old Serbs ate only venison, while keeping the livestock for use in agriculture. Nowadays much has changed, but the traditions have not been abandoned.

Voivodinian cuisine is recognizable for its goulashes, stews and various sorts of meat products and delicacies. Shumadiya is well known for its steaks and roast pork, while Western Serbia excells in dried meat. When you visit the mountains of Zlatibor and Zlatar, you should not miss lamb dishes and local kaymak. The cuisine of Eastern Serbia is recognizable by lamb cooked in milk, dried boar meat, and yaniyas made of three different types of meat and various vegetables...

SAUERKRAUT SARMA

INGREDIENTS:
3.3–4.4 lb (1.5–2 kg) of sauerkraut
1 tablespoon of fat, onion
1½ lb (700 g) of mixed ground meat
1 cup of rice, 9 oz (250 g) of dry ribs
5 oz (150 g) of dry bacon
4–5 bay leaves
1 tablespoon of fat, tablespoon of flour
1 teaspoon of cayenne pepper

RECIPE:
The best cabbage for sarmas is „melezan" (crossbread), with medium size head and densely crowded, thin leaves. Take a pickled cabbage head, remove the leaves, and thin the hard vein using a knife. If the cabbage is too acidic, rinse it with cold water. Take a pot, heat a tablespoon of fat, and add one finely chopped onion and 700 g (1½ lb) of mixed minced meat. When the meat is fried, add a cup of rice, a little cayenne pepper, black pepper and salt to taste. In a larger pot arrange several cabbage leaves. How to wrap a sarma: take a larger leaf, cut it in half, put a little filling on it, than fold the sides, wrap and tuck the part that is sticking out. Arrange sarmas one next to the other in the pot, in several layers. Between the sarmas insert 250 g (9 oz) of dry ribs and 150 g (5 oz) of chopped smoked bacon, a few black peppercorns, and a couple of bay leaves. Pour water until the sarmas are submerged, and cook at a low heat for 3–4 hours. When the sarmas are cooked, pour over them a browned flour which you prepare this way: one tablespoon of flour place on a tablespoon of heated fat, add a teaspoon of cayenne pepper, and fry while stirring. Pour it on the sarmas, and leave to simmer for another half an hour.

LAMB SARMA

INGREDIENTS:
   1 tablespoon of fat
   3–4 spring onions
   1 lamb peritoneum
   1 lamb black liver
   1 lamb white liver
   1 lamb heart
   A pinch of parsley, 3 eggs
   Milk, pepper and salt as needed

RECIPE:

Heat a tablespoon of fat in a pan, add a couple of spring onions, roughly chopped. Add diced lamb liver, black and white, and lamb heart. Fry it all together, add salt, pepper and finely chopped parsley, and remove from heat. There are two ways you can make sarmas: cut pieces of lamb peritoneum, wrap sarmas the same way you wrap a sauerkraut sarma, and then arrange them in a baking pan, one next to another; or you can put the stuffing in the middle of lamb peritoneum, wrap it carefully, and put one big sarma in a baking pan. Whatever option you choose, you should beat 3 eggs, add a little milk, salt to taste, pour water over it, and put to bake.

LITTLE SARMAS WITH KALE AND MEAT

INGREDIENTS:
  2 lb (1 kg) of kale
  1 lb (½ kg) of ground meat
  7 oz (200 ml) of sour cream
  7 oz (200 g) of kaymak
  Salt and pepper as needed

RECIPE:
Clean 1 kg (2 lb) of kale, separate its leaves, and parboil them in hot water. Put ½ kg (1 lb) of meat in heated oil and, when fried, add 200 ml (7 oz) of sour cream and 200 g (7 oz) of kaymak, then season with salt and pepper. Stir and remove from heat. Drain cale leaves, fill them with stuffing and wrap the same way you wrap the sauerkraut sarmas. Arrange them in a fireproof casserole, pour water, and bake in the oven until brown.

STUFFED PEPPERS IN TOMATO SAUCE

Ingredients:

    10 fresh green peppers
    5 tablespoons of red soy flakes
    1 onion, 1 cup of rice, 1 carrot
    1 lb (½ kg) of ground meat
    5 fl oz (150 ml) of lukewarm water
    7 fl oz (200 ml) of ground tomatoes
    2 tablespoons of flour
    Cayenne pepper, salt and pepper as
    needed

Recipe:

Take 10 green peppers, wash them, remove stems. Arrange them upright in a pot. Soak 5 tablespoons of red soy flakes in a bowl. Take another bowl, grate one onion and one carrot, then add ½ kg (1 lb) of ground meat, a little cayenne pepper, salt, pepper, a cup of rice and soaked soy flakes. Stir all well together and then stuff peppers with the filling. Pour water over them until they are submerged, and then put on a low heat to simmer. After an hour, in the water around the peppers pour tomato sauce, which is prepared like this: in 150 ml (5 fl oz) of lukewarm water and 200 ml (7 fl oz) of tomato sauce stir 2 tablespoons of flour. Shake the pan to evenly distribute the sauce, and let simmer for another 10 minutes.

LAMB KAPAMA WITH DOCK LEAVES

Ingredients:

    1 ½ kb (700 g) of lamb
    2 leeks
    2 bunches of spring onions
    2 onions
    1 clove of garlic
    3.5 fl oz (100 ml) of white wine
    4 bunches of dock leaves
    Parsley, salt and sour milk as needed

Recipe:

Take 700 g (1½ lb) of meat from the lamb leg, dice it, roll in flour and fry in hot oil until golden brown. Remove the pieces of meat and in the same oil stew 2 sliced leeks, 2 chopped onions, 2 bunches of spring onions and a clove of garlic. Onions and garlic together should not be heavier than ½ kg (1 lb). When they soften, add lamb, 100 ml (3.5 fl oz) of white wine, some parsley and seasoning to taste; pour water until all the ingredients are submerged, then leave to simmer for half an hour, stirring occasionally. If necessary, add more water, but be careful, because the dish should not be neither watery nor too thick. In the meantime, wash 4 bunches of dock leaves, remove the stalks with a knife, and flatten the leaf veins. Cut the leaves into thick strips, submerge them in the boiling water for a minute, and then leave to drain. When the meat is prepared, add dock leaves and some salt, if needed, stir it all together, and leave to simmer for a couple of minutes. Kapama is served with sour milk.

BEANS WITH DRY PORK

INGREDIENTS:
- 1 lb (½ kg) of beans
- 2 onions
- 1– 1 ½ lb (500–700 g) of dry ribs
- 10 grains of pepper
- 2 bay leaves
- 1 tablespoon of flour
- 1 teaspoon of cayenne pepper
- Salt and oil as needed

RECIPE:
Wash ½ kg (1 lb) of beans and drop into the pot. Pour cold water over until they are submerged, and put on the stove to boil. When boiled, throw away the water, then pour fresh water, add two finely chopped onions, 500–700 g (1–1½ lb) of dry ribs, 10 peppercorns, 2 bay leaves. Cook the beans for 2–3 hours. When they soften, add some salt if necessary, because ribs themselves are salty. In the end, add some browned flour, which you will prepare this way: put one tablespoon of flour in the heated oil and fry until it is brown. Add 2–3 chopped cloves of garlic, fry briefly, remove from heat, season with a teaspoon of cayenne pepper and pour it into the beans. Let the pot simmer for another 10 minutes, so the flavors merge.

STEWED SAUERKRAUT WITH TURKEY

INGREDIENTS:
4.4 lb (2 kg) of turkey
3.5 oz (100 g) of fat
1 onion
5.5 lb (2.5 kg) of sauerkraut
2 cloves of garlic
2 bay leaves
Pepper as nedeed

RECIPE:
Salt a turkey of up to 2 kg (4.4 lb) weight, stuff its cavity with 100 g (3.5 oz) of fat and then sew it. Bake at medium heat for 2–3 hours. During cooking, pour over water mixed with fat, which you can keep on the stove, so it remains warm. In a pan with heated grease drop one finely chopped onion, and then add 2,5 kg (5.5 lb) of sauerkraut cut into strips, and a little water. Leave to stew over a low heat. Occasionally pour in some water, so the sauerkraut does not burn, and cook it until it softens. Remove turkey from the casserole, then put the sauerkraut in it. Add some pepper, 2 cloves of chopped garlic, 2 bay leaves, and stir all together. Place the turkey on the sauerkraut, and return to oven. Bake for another 20 minutes, until water evaporates from the sauerkraut and it becomes darker.

WEDDING SAUERKRAUT

INGREDIENTS:
    Mixed meat
    Sauerkraut
    Bacon
    Dry ribs
    Onions
    Bay leaves
    Black pepper
    Cayenne pepper

RECIPE:

This dish is cooked for hours in a clay pot, and for it you will need almost the same amounts of meat and sauerkraut. At the bottom of a pot arrange diced bacon, put some roughly chopped sauerkraut over it, then a layer of diced and mixed pork, veal and sheep meat, along with smoked ribs, bacon, chopped onions, 2–3 bay leaves, pepper and cayenne pepper. Drop the sauerkraut over the meat, and build up layers until all the ingredients are used up, ensuring that sauerkraut forms the top layer. Pour over cold water, until all is submerged, and allow to simmer for 4–5 hours on medium heat. Do not stir, but shake the pot occasionally. Serve with cornbread.

EGGPLANT MOUSSAKA

Ingredients:
    4 eggplants
    1 lb (½ kg) of beef
    ½ lb (¼ kg) of pork
    1 onion, 1 fresh green pepper
    2–3 tomatoes
    3 eggs
    7 oz (200 ml) of sour cream
    Parsley, salt, pepper and flour as needed

Recipe:
Peel 4 bigger eggplants, cut lengthwise into thin slices, arrange in a pot and season with salt. Let them sit like this for at least one hour. In the meanwhile, grind ½ kg (1 lb) of beef, and ¼ kg (½ lb) of pork. In a pan with heated fat fry one chopped onion, sliced green pepper, 2–3 sliced tomatoes and a little parsley. Drop the meat into the pan, and continue frying. Remove the pan from heat and add some salt, pepper and one egg to the meat, and stir it all together. Drain the sliced eggplants, rool them first in flour, then in beaten eggs and, finally, in bread crumbs, and fry in fat until golden brown on both sides. In a fireproof dish arrange a layer of eggplants, and pour over beaten eggs mixed with sour cream; then comes a layer of meat, which you will also top with eggs. Continue building up layers, until you have used all the ingredients, while ensuring that the final one is formed by eggplants thoroughly topped with beaten eggs. Bake the moussaka in the oven until it gets a crust.

POTATO MOUSSAKA

INGREDIENTS:
  1 lb (½ kg) of mixed ground meat
  3.3 lb (1.5 kg) of potatoes
  2 onions
  2 eggs
  1 cup of milk
  Salt and pepper as needed

RECIPE:
Fry two finely chopped onions in heated oil, add ½ kg (1 lb) of mixed ground meat, season with salt and pepper, and continue frying until the water from the meat has evaporated. Put 1,5 kg (3.3 lb) of potatoes in hot water. When boiled, peel them and cut into thin slices. Take a fireproof dish, and arrange the ingredients like this: one layer of potatoes, one layer of meat, until you have used them all. Ensure that potatoes form the top layer. Beat two eggs with a cup of milk, pour them over the potatoes, and bake at higher heat until the crust forms.

CHICKEN PILAV

INGREDIENTS:
   4 chicken breast fillets
   1 cup of mushrooms
   1 cup of peas
   2 cups of rice
   1 onion
   Chicken soup, salt and
   pepper as needed

RECIPE:
Take 4 chicken breast fillets and fry them in heated oil. A cup of chopped mushrooms drop in the pan, as well as a cup of peas and two cups of rice, a smaller head of chopped onion, and then pour hot chicken soup over it all. Season with salt and pepper, and top it with chicken meat. Boil at a low heat until the rice has softened.

CHICKEN IN DOUGH

INGREDIENTS:
  2 onions
  1 carrot
  ½ celery stalk
  1 chicken
  ½ glass of white wine, and the same
  amount of water
  5 eggs

RECIPE:

Chop a lot of onion and drop it in heated fat, then add a carrot and some celery. While the onion is being fried, clean the chicken, cut it into pieces, season with salt and put in the pan with vegetables. Let them fry together until the chicken turns yellow. Pour half a glass of white wine and some water, add a little pepper and salt, and stew until the meat has completely softened. In the meantime, make the dough: beat five egg whites until soft peaks form, stir in egg yolks (one at a time!), then add five tablespoons of flour, and stir it well together. Place the chicken in a fireproof dish, pour over the sauce in which it was cooked, and coat with dough, so the whole chicken is covered. Put it into the oven, and wait for the dough to bake.

CHICKEN STEW WITH DUMPLINGS

Ingredients:
1 chicken
1 lb (½ kg) of onions
1 fresh green pepper
4–5 tomatoes, 2 eggs
1 tablespoon of fat
2–3 tablespoons of flour
Cayenne pepper, salt,
parsley and pepper as needed

Recipe:
Wash chicken and cut it into pieces. Clean ½ kg (1 lb) of onions, cut them into rings, season with salt and drop in hot fat to fry. Add a pinch of cayenne pepper, one green pepper and the meat, and fry it all together until the onions are completely fried. Then pour water until the meat is submerged, add 4–5 sliced tomatoes, a little parsley, and pepper and salt, if necessary. Reduce heat and simmer the stew, stirring occasionally, until almost all water has evaporated. Chicken stew you may serve with dumplings which are made this way: put 2 egg yolks, a level tablespoon of fat, some salt, 2 beaten egg whites in a bowl, add the flour, and whisk everything together. Put some water in a pan, salt it, and then with a spoon, which you should regularly douse in hot water, remove small balls of dough and place them in boiling water. If dumplings fall apart first, it means that you should add more flour. Boiled dumplings will rise to the top, so you remove them with slotted spoon and drain well. Pour dumplings in the middle of a dish, arrange meat around them, and top it all with the stew sauce.

VENISON STEW

INGREDIENTS:
    1.75 pt (1 l) of water
    1 pt (½ l) of white wine
    1.75 pt (1 l) of winegar
    1 bunch of greens, 2 bay leaves
    3 cloves of garlic, 28 oz (800 g) of venison
    7 fl oz (200 ml) of white wine
    7 fl 07 (200 ml) of sour cream
    Salt and pepper as needed

RECIPE:
Mix one liter (1.75 pt) of water with ½ l (0.9 pt) of white wine and 1 liter (1.75 pt) of vinegar. Add a bunch of chopped white and orange carrots, 2 bay leaves, 3 cloves of garlic, a little pepper and salt, and let it cook. When it boils, remove from heat to cool down, and then put 800 g (28 oz) of venison in it. Meat should stand in the marinade for at least 2 days before use. Then you remove it from the marinade, and cut into smaller pieces. Chop 2 white and 2 orange carrots, as well as 2 onions, dice the venison, put all of these in hot oil, and let stew. Occasionally pour 200 ml (7 fl oz) of white wine. When the meat has softened, remove it from the pot, mash the vegetables, season with salt and pepper, and then return to the pot, while adding 200 ml (7 oz) of sour cream. Simmer over low heat so it does not burn, occasionally pouring water, if necessary. Then return the meat to the pot, and simmer over low heat for a while.

VOIVODINIAN SEKELI GOULASH

INGREDIENTS:
- 2 lb (1 kg) of pork
- 4 onions
- 2 lb (1 kg) of grated sauerkraut
- 7 fl oz (200 ml) of sour cream
- Salt, pepper and cayenne pepper as needed

RECIPE:

Wash 1 kg (2 lb) of pork leg and cut it into small cubes. Clean and chop 2 onions and drop them into the hot fat. Place 1 kg (2 lb) of grated sauerkraut on the onions, ensuring that the sauerkraut is previously washed to remove excess acid. Fry them together, stirring often. In a separate pan heat some fat, drop 2 chopped onions and cut pork. When the meat has completely softened, and the cabbage stewed, add some cayenne pepper, salt and pepper, top it all with 200 ml (7 oz) of sour cream, and leave to simmer for a short while.

LESKOVAC JUMBLE (MUĆKALICA)

INGREDIENTS:
20 oz (600 g) of lean pork
14 oz (400 g) of bacon
3–4 onions, 1 head of garlic
½ of hot little pepper
6–7 roasted peppers
2–3 tomatoes
4–5 tablespoons of ayvar
1 tablespoon of cayenne pepper

RECIPE:
Take 600 g (21 oz) of the best lean pork, cut it into pieces, season with salt, and leave to rest for 10 minutes. On each piece of meat put a cube of bacon, thread them on little skewers and grill. In the meantime, stew 3–4 chopped onions at a low heat. When half fried, add a chopped head of garlic and a half of hot pepper. Then add, one by one: 6–7 roasted, peeled and chopped bell peppers, 2–3 peeled tomatoes, 4–5 tablespoons of ayvar, 6–7 roasted and peeled peppers, and a tablespoon of cayenne pepper. Stew all the ingredients on a low heat for about 15 minutes, then pour in a fireproof casserole. Gently dip the meat in the vegetables, and place into the oven, on a higher heat, to brown.

SERBIAN DJUVETCH

INGREDIENTS:
    2 lb (1 kg) of young onions
    1 lb (½ kg) of pork
    3–4 tomatoes, 3–4 new potatoes
    1 eggplant, 1 zucchini
    2–3 fresh green peppers
    A pinch of parsley, a pinch of celery leaf
    1 cup of rice, 1 tablespoon of fat
    Salt and pepper as needed

RECIPE:
Take 1 kg (2 lb) of young onions and cut them into thin strips, then put in a deeper dish. Add a few tomatoes, cut in slices, 3–4 young potatoes, one diced eggplant, one diced zucchini, 2–3 chopped long green peppers, some parsley, one celery leaf and a cup of rice; then season with salt and pepper, and add the pork cut into chunks. Mix all ingredients, place them in a fireproof dish and top with a few tomato slices. Add a large spoonful of fat, pour water until the vegetables are submerged, and bake for at least 3 hours, because djuvetch should not be too brothy, but well stewed.

ROASTED PORK

INGREDIENTS:
  1 pig
  1–2 glasses of water
  Beer and salt as needed

RECIPE:
Salt the pork and put it on the slats, so it does not touch the bottom of a baking pan. Pour 1–2 glasses of water and bake with high heat for 15 minutes. Reduce heat significantly and, brushing the pork with beer, bake in the oven for 4–6 hours.

TRIPE

INGREDIENTS:
    2 lb (1 kg) of tripe
    1–2 onions, 1–2 carrots
    4–5 tomatoes
    4 cloves of garlic
    2 bay leaves
    1 tablespoon of flour
    A pinch of cayenne pepper
    Salt and parsley as needed

RECIPE:
Take 1 kg (2 lb) of tripe, wash and cook for about 3 hours in salted water. When cooled, cut the tripe into strips. Fry in hot oil 1–2 chopped onions, 1–2 diced carrots, 4–5 milled tomatoes, chopped 4 cloves of garlic, 2 bay leaves, salt, parsley and cooked tripe. Then pour more lukewarm water, and leave to simmer. Towards the end, add browned flour, which you make like this: put a tablespoon of flour in hot oil and, when it gets a little browner, add a pinch of cayenne pepper, and stir well while frying.

KARADJORDJE'S STEAK

INGREDIENTS:
   1 lb (½ kg) young beef steaks
   7 oz (200 g) of kaymak
   Salt, eggs and bread crumbs
   as needed

RECIPE:
Beat well ½ kg (1 lb) of young beef steaks, season with salt, fill each one with kaymak, roll and fasten with toothpicks. When prepared, roll them first in beaten eggs, then in bread crumbs, and fry in hot oil until golden brown. Remove toothpicks and serve with mashed potatoes or French fries.

HUNTER'S SCHNITZEL

INGREDIENTS:
  1 lb (½ kg) of beef steaks
  1 tablespoon of fat
  1 bay leaf
  3.5 fl oz (100 ml) of sour cream
  Eggs, ham, salt, flour and pepper
  as needed

RECIPE:
Beat well 1 kg (2 lb) of young beef steaks, season with salt, roll each one in flour, and fry in fat. Take as many eggs as you have steaks and fry them in a saucepan. On each steak put an egg, a piece of thinly sliced ham, roll and fasten with toothpicks. Put a tablespoon of fat in a fireproof vessel, and place the rolled steaks in it. Add a little water, season with pepper and bay leaf, and bake the schnitzels in the oven. After a while, add 100 ml (3.5 oz) of sour cream, and return the meat into the oven, until it softens completely. Remove toothpicks, arrange schnitzels on a platter, and top it with the sauce in which they were baked.

BEEF IN TOMATO SAUCE

INGREDIENTS:
    6 tomatoes
    2 heads of garlic
    1 tablespoon of fat
    1 tablespoon of flour
    A pinch of cayenne
    1.7 oz (50 g) of cooked ham
    1 lb (½ kg) of beef
    Grated cheese, celery, salt
    and pepper as needed

RECIPE:
Peel and slice 6 tomatoes, chop 2 cloves of garlic, add some celery, season with salt and pepper, and stew it all on a tablespoon of fat. In another vessel, fry a tablespoon of flour, with a pinch of cayenne pepper, then add the stewed tomatoes, and pour a little water. Then add 50 g (1.7 oz) of chopped cooked ham, and let it boil for 10 minutes. In the meantime, chop ½ kg (1 lb) of beef, season with salt and pepper, fry a little, and place in a fireproof dish, then pour the tomato sauce over it, sprinkle with grated cheese, and bake in the oven, with low heat, until the flavors merge.

METOHIAN PAN

INGREDIENTS:
   3.3 lb (1,5 kg) of lamb meat
   3 eggs
   3.5 fl oz (1 dcl) of sour milk
   Kaymak, salt and parsley
   as needed

RECIPE:

Take 1,5 kg (3.3 lb) of lamb meat, cut it into thicker steaks, season with salt, and arrange in an oiled pan, coated with kaymak (round casserole or clay pot). Then coat the meat with kaymak, and bake. Towards the end, top it with a mixture of 3 beaten eggs and 1 dl (3.5 fl oz) of sour milk, sprinkle with parsley, and return to the oven, so the eggs turn brown.

LAMB COOKED IN MILK

INGREDIENTS:

   2 lb (1 kg) of lamb meat
   1.75 pt (1 l) of milk
   3.3 lb (1,5 kg) of potatoes
   2 tablespoons of kaymak
   1 sprig of rosemary
   Salt and pepper as needed

RECIPE:

One kilogram (2 lb) of lamb meat place in one liter (1.75 pt) of milk, and let it sit for 2 hours. Rub salt into the meat, add a few bay leaves, a sprig of rosemary, and fry in a large casserole. Half roasted lamb place in a fireproof dish, arrange around it 1,5 kg (3.3 lb) of roughly cut and salted potatoes, pour some oil over and add 2 tablespoons of kaymak. Bake at low heat for about an hour and a half.

LAMB KAPAMA

INGREDIENTS:
> A front or rear quarter of a lamb
> 1 lb (½ kg) of onions
> 4 bunches of spring onions
> 7 oz (200 g) of spinach
> A pinch of cayenne pepper
> Pepper and salt as needed

RECIPE:
A front or rear quarter of lamb cut into smaller pieces. Wash the meat, season it with salt, roll into flour, and fry in fat until golden brown. Remove the meat, and in the same fat place ½ kg (1 lb) of chopped onions and 4 bunches of spring onions. In a half fried onions add meat, and fry it together for a little while. Then add a pinch of cayenne pepper, pour the soup or water until the meat is submerged, season with salt and pepper, and stew on a low heat. When finished, serve with sour milk.

ROASTED LAMB

INGREDIENTS:
¼ of a lamb
White wine, water,
rosemary and salt as needed

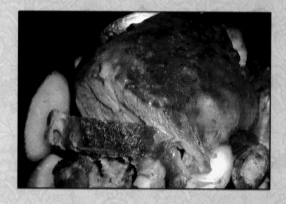

RECIPE:
Wash, dry and incise the meat in several places, so it better absorbs spices, then season with salt, thoroughly rubbing it in. Mix a small amounts of water, white wine and rosemary, and pour the mixture in a casserole in which you will roast the meat. Place the lamb in the casserole, cover it with the baking aluminium foil, and bake with moderate heat, turning it occasionally and brushing with its own juice. Towards the end, remove the foil and leave the meat in the oven for another 15 minute, until a nice brown crust forms.

Grilled Dishes

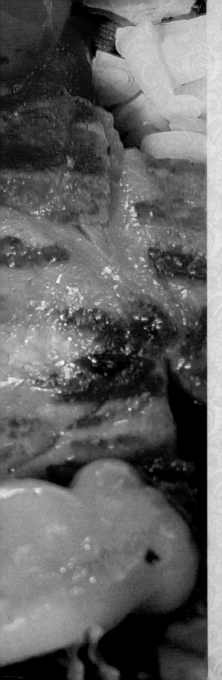

Serbian grilled specialties have become a symbol of traditional cuisine, especially the famous *ćevapčići*, grilled meat dumplings (minced meat shaped in fingers and roasted on a grill).

The highlight of grilled delights certainly is grilled mixed meat, made of several kinds of meat specialties: *ćevapčići*, pljeskavice (burgers), meat fritters, sausages, steaks, little skewers... Widely known is the so-called „Leskovac Train"; how many „wagons" this train will have, depends strictly on your appetite... You took 2–3 ćevapčića, then comes the burger; you still didn't have time to reach for the glass, when a hot sausage arrives... With the homemade flat bread (*lepinja*) and salads – you, and no one but you shall determine which wagon will be the last!

The tradition of preserving meat by smoking led many restaurant owners and chefs to incorporate thus prepared meats in their menus. The most famous is smoked *vešalica* – smoked pork carré with a healthy Serbian salad. Have we missed something? Well, yes: enjoy a glass of high-quality red wine.

CEVAPCICI

INGREDIENTS:
  1 lb (½ kg) of pork
  1 lb (½ kg) of young beef
  7 fl oz (2 dcl) of mineral water
  2 teaspoons of baking soda
  3 tablespoons of onion powder
  3 tablespoons of garlic powder
  Butter, salt and pepper as needed

RECIPE:
Mixture for cevapcici should be prepared the day before frying. Mix ½ kg (1 lb) of beef and the same amount of pork ground meat, season with salt and pepper, and knead for at least 5 minutes. In a separate bowl mix 2 dl (7 fl oz) of mineral water, 2 teaspoons of baking soda, 3 tablespoons of onion powder and 3 tablespoons of garlic powder. Add some mineral water, and knead for a long time. Return the meat to the fridge and leave overnight. Shape the meat with a special funnel, or with your oiled hands. Before frying, grease a pan or a grill using a piece of butter.

PLIESKAVITZA (BURGER) WITH KAYMAK

INGREDIENTS:

    2 lb (1 kg) mixed ground meat
    5 fl oz (1,5 dl) of mineral water
    1 tablespoon of baking soda
    3 tablespoons of onion powder
    3 tablespoons of garlic powder
    1 tablespoon of kaymak
    Salt and pepper as needed

RECIPE:

Take 1 kg (2 lb) of mixed ground meat, season with salt and pepper, and knead thoroughly. In a separate bowl pour 1,5 dl (5 fl oz) of mineral water, a tablespoon of baking soda, 3 tablespoons of onion powder and 3 tablespoons of garlic powder. Add this mixture to the meat, knead for a long time, and then leave in the fridge for at least 5 hours. With your hands oiled, shape the plieskavitzas (burgers), and place one by one in hot oil. Towards the end of frying, put a tablespoon of kaymak to melt on each plieskavitza. Serve with new potatoes or French fries, and tomato salad with spring onions.

LITTLE SKEWERS

INGREDIENTS:
2 lb (1 kg) of pork
Onion and salt as needed

RECIPE:
First you should prepare wooden sticks, about 20 cm (8 in) long, half a centimeter (0,2 in) thick, pointed on one side. About half an hour before use, put them into the water, so they don't burn easily. Then take 1 kg (2 lb) of white pork tenderloin, wash it and cut into pieces 7–10 cm (3–4 in) long, and season with salt. Thread the pieces of meat, together with slices of onion and peppers, on the skewers, alternating them as you do. Oil the grill before you start cooking.

LESKOVAC FRITTERS

Ingredients:
2 lb (1 kg) of mixed ground meat
5 oz (150) of dried bacon
5 oz (150 g) of kashkaval cheese
2 tablespoons of cayenne pepper
5–6 cloves of garlic
Salt and pepper as needed

Recipe:
Take 1 kg (2 lb) of mixed minced meat and mix it with 150 g (5 oz) of chopped smoked bacon and 150 g (5 oz) of finely shredded kashkaval cheese. Add 2 tablespoons of cayenne pepper, 5–6 chopped garlic, some pepper and salt. Knead all well, and leave in the fridge for at least one hour. Take the pieces of the prepared meat with greased hands, and shape them into fritters (balls). Grill 7–8 minutes, and serve with chopped onion or salad of roasted peppers with garlic.

PORK RIB EYE STEAK IN PERITONEUM

INGREDIENTS:
  6 pork rib eye steaks
  1 pig peritoneum
  Salt and ground hot pepper
  as needed

RECIPE:
Take 6 pork rib eye steaks (krmenadle), season with salt and minced hot pepper, and beat the meat well. Wrap each steak in pig peritoneum, and grill until golden brown on both sides. Rib eye steaks serve with chopped onion and warm flatbread or bannock.

Freshwater Fish Dishes

natural beauty certainly is one of the greatest treasures of Serbia. The country is intersected by beautiful rivers winding through breathtaking canyons and gorges. Many centuries have passed since the local nature lovers began building the *chardas*, tucked in the woods near the rivers. *Chardas* are usually located outside the populated areas, and offer the best freshwater fish meals, as well as the high-quality wines and brandies made of indigenous varieties of grapes from throughout the region.

The fresh smell of this part of Europe, the aroma of stews and fish specialties, represents a true cure for all the stresses of modern life. So, when you decide to go to a *charda*, that means that you're finally up to devote little attention to yourself. Water soothes the soul, they say, and people who spend their lives near the rivers are a world for themselves. Fishing every day, they also earn a living, and the hot fish soup and fish stew they make – cannot be found elsewhere, even if you travelled up the Danube to Buda and Pest...

FISH STEW

INGREDIENTS:

- 2 lb (1 kg) of onions
- 2 carrots
- 10 grains of pepper
- 2 chili peppers, 2 bay leaves
- 2 tablespoons of tomato purée
- 7 fl oz (2 dcl) of white wine
- 2 lb (1 kg) of mixed fish
- Salt and pepper as needed

RECIPE:

Heat some oil to a medium temperature, and drop 1 kg (2 lb) of finely chopped onions into it. Add 2 diced carrots, a dozen of peppercorns, 2 chopped chili peppers, a bay leaf, and stew about an hour, occasionally adding water. Season with salt, add 2 tablespoons of tomato purée, 2 dl (7 fl oz) of white wine, and cook for another 15 minutes. Take 1 kg (2 lb) of mixed fish (perch, carp, sterlet, catfish). Clean the fish, cut them into pieces, put in the pan with vegetables and allow to simmer for 20 minutes. Add water if necessary. In the end, add some cayenne pepper and cook for 10 minutes.

UZICE STYLE TROUT

INGREDIENTS:
- 1.75 lb (800 g) of trouts
- 5.5 oz (160 g) of bacon
- 1 lb (½ kg) of new (young) potatoes
- 7 oz (200 g) of kaymak
- Flour, parsley and salt as needed

RECIPE:
Clean, wash and dry 4 trouts, each weighing about 200 g (7 oz). Cut 160 g (5.5 oz) of bacon into thin slices and fry. Take ½ kg (1 lb) of new (young) potatoes, peeled them and boil in salted water. Roll the trouts in flour, and fry over low heat in the fat in which the bacon was previously cooked. Arrange the fish on a platter, covering the bacon, and top with fat in which they were fried. Add those boiled potatoes, pour over 200 g (7 oz) of melted kaymak, and sprinkle with parsley.

SMOKED TROUT

INGREDIENTS:
  ½ glass of white wine
  ½ glass of water
  1 lemon
  4 cloves of garlic
  2 lb (1 kg) of smoked trout
  Salt as needed

RECIPE:

In a bowl, mix half a glass of white wine, half a glas of water, juice of one lemon, 4 cloves of finely chopped garlic, season with salt and leave to sit for 15 minutes. Strain into a pan, add some oil, heat it on the stove, and put 1 kg (2 lb) of washed and cleaned smoked trout. Simmer until the liquid evaporates. Serve with potato salad.

DRUNKEN CARP

INGREDIENTS:
7 fl oz (2 dcl) of white wine
1 head of garlic
4.4 lb (2 kg) of carp
1 lb (1/2 kg) of rice
1 onion
Parsley and salt as needed

RECIPE:
In a deeper dish pour 2 dl (7 fl oz) of white wine, add a clove of grated garlic, and season with salt. Put a carp weighing 2 kg (4.4 lb), washed and cleaned, in the marinade, and leave it submerged for at least half an hour. Transfer it to a baking pan and cook on high heat for 15 minutes. In the meantime, mildly fry ½ kg (1 lb) of rice adding one chopped onion, pour water over, season with salt and, constantly stirring, simmer it for a couple of minutes, before finally adding some parsley. Remove the carp from the oven, arrange rice around, baste with the marinade, and bake for up to an hour on high heat.

STUFFED CARP

INGREDIENTS:

3.5–4 lb (1,5–2 kg) of carp
1 onion
2 heads of garlic
1 carrot
3.5 oz (100 g) of meaty bacon
3.5 oz (100 g) of rice

RECIPE:

Wash and clean the carp weighing 2 kg (4 lb), cut it on both sides, in several places, and season with salt. In a pan with hot oil put one chopped onion, 2 cloves of garlic, one chopped carrot, a little chopped meaty bacon, 100 g (3.5 oz) of rice, then pour the water and cook. With this stuffing fill the carp, fasten with toothpicks, and bake on medium heat for an hour. During roasting, baste with white wine.

CARP WITH PRUNES

INGREDIENTS:
    4.4 lb (2 kg) of carp
    2 onions
    1 cup of rice
    3 cups of cube soup
    Flour, parsley, salt and pepper as needed

RECIPE:
A carp weighing up to 2 kg (4,4 lb) wash and clean, season with salt, roll in flour, and fry briefly in hot oil. In another dish, fry 2 smaller chopped onions, add a cup of rice and 3 cups of cube soup. When it boils, season with salt and pepper, add some parsley and 20 pitted prunes. Leave it over heat for a short while, then pour to a fireproof dish, place the carp into it, and cook on higher temperature until golden brown.

PIKEPERCH WITH MUSHROOMS AND GRATED CHEESE

INGREDIENTS:
2 lb (1 kg) of pikeperch
7 oz (200 g) of mushrooms
7 fl oz (200 ml) of sour cream
Grated cheese, salt and
parsley as needed

RECIPE:
Wash, clean and dry 1 kg (2 lb) of pikeperch. Cut the fish into pieces, season with salt, and fry until golden brown on both sides. Wash and boil 200 g (7 oz) of mushrooms, drain them, add salt and mix with 200 ml (7 oz) of sour cream and a pinch of parsley. Pieces of fried pikeperch arrange in a fireproof dish, top with prepared sauce, sprinkle with grated cheese, and bake in the oven briefly, until the cheese is golden brown.

PIKEPERCH CHOPS

INGREDIENTS:
   2 lb (1 kg) of pikeperch
   1 lemon
   7 fl oz (200 ml) of yogurt
   3.5 oz (100 g) of mayonnaise
   1 tablespoon of parsley
   1 tablespoon of dill
   Salt and pepper as needed

RECIPE:
Wash and clean 1 kg (2 lb) of pikeperch, finely chop the fish, then baste each piece with lemon juice, and season with salt and pepper. Mix 200 ml (7 fl oz) of yogurt with 100 g (3.5 oz) of mayonnaise, a tablespoon of finely chopped parsley and the same amount of dill. Roll the fish in flour and fry on hot oil, until both sides are golden brown. Arrange the fried fish in a platter, top with prepared sauce and garnish with lemon rings.

PIKEPERCH CROQUETTES

INGREDIENTS:
  2 lb (1 kg) of pikeperch
  2 carrots
  1 lemon
  10 mushrooms
  3.5 oz (100 g) of margarine
  2 tomatoes
  Salt and flour as needed

RECIPE:
Wash, clean and cut into pieces 1 kg (2 lb) of pikeperch. Boil the head and the tail in salted water, adding a bunch of greens. Get the cut pieces cleaned of bones, and then fry them in a little oil. Transfer them to another dish, pour in juice of one lemon, and set aside to cool. In the oil in which the fish was fried, place a dozen chopped mushrooms, fry them, and pour the oil out. In a deeper dish, heat 100 g (3.5 oz) of margarine, add flour as needed, season with salt, and pour strained broth to obtain a thicker sauce. Boil and mash 2 potatoes, put them in the sauce, stir and then add the pieces of fried pikeperch and mushrooms. With a spoon, gently lower the croquettes into the oil and fry until golden brown. Serve them with green salad.

BREADED STERLET

INGREDIENTS:
  2 lb (1 kg) of sterlet
  1 lemon
  Eggs, flour, bread crumbs
  and salt as needed

RECIPE:
Scald 2 lb (1 kg) of sterlet, remove from water, peel the fish, and take out the intestines as well as the vein along the spine. Wash, cut into pieces, dry, dip with lemon juice and season with salt. Thus prepared fish roll first in flour, then in scrambled eggs and, finally, in bread crumbs, and fry until golden brown.

ROASTED STERLET

INGREDIENTS:
  2 lb (1 kg) of sterlet
  2 lemons
  3.5 oz (100 g) of butter
  Potatoes, parsley and salt
  as needed

RECIPE:

Scald 2 lb (1 kg) of sterlet, remove from water, peel the fish, and take out the intestines as well as the vein along the spine. Season with salt, arrange in a baking pan, top with melted butter, sprinkle with parsley, and cook at mild temperature for up to one hour. Arrange roasted sterlet on a plate, and top it with the juice of 2 lemons mixed with the juice in which the fish was cooked. Then add the boiled potatoes sprinkled with parsley.

CATFISH IN SOUR CREAM SAUCE

INGREDIENTS:
    2 lb (1 kg) of catfish
    4–5 tomatoes
    1 leek
    13.5 oz (400 ml) of sour cream
    1 head of garlic
    1 teaspoon of cayenne pepper
    Flour, parsley and salt as needed

RECIPE:
Wash and clean 1 kg (2 lb) of catfish, cut it into pieces, season with salt, roll in flour, and fry in hot oil until golden brown. Boil 4–5 potatoes, chop them and fry with leek. In a smaller dish, mix 400 ml (13.5 oz) of sour cream, a clove of chopped garlic, one teaspoon of cayenne pepper, finely chopped parsley, and salt to taste. In a fireproof dish arrange the fried potatoes and catfish, top with sour cream, and cook on a higher heat for about half an hour.

Salads

In Serbia, salads are eaten with meals. Once upon a time, people consumed strictly seasonal salads. During winter, it was pickles, or *turšija* (sour cabbage and a variety of pickled vegetables), and in the summer, of course, fresh vegetables.

However, this division is not relevant today. Tomatoes, peppers, onions and hot little peppers are the most common ingredients in mixed salads all year round.

Do not be surprised if you are offered a drink as soon as the salad is served – a homemade plum brandy. Cabbage goes well with a quality brandy *prepečenica*.

In addition to salads mentioned above, you can also get a salad of fresh cabbage, boiled beets, lettuce, beans and green beans, celery, potatoes... In accordance with old traditions, on the tables in some restaurants you will find fresh, green, hot little peppers, or roasted peppers with garlic in oil, as a sign of welcome.

COLESLAW

INGREDIENTS:
 1 head of sweet cabbage
 Salt, pepper, oil, vinegar
 and parsley as needed

RECIPE:
Chop a head of sweet cabbage into thin strips, after you have removed outer leaves and root. Season with salt and leave to stand for some time. Drain the water, add some pepper, oil and vinegar, mix it all well, sprinkle with parsley, and serve.

SERBIAN SALAD

INGREDIENTS:
    5 oz (150 g) of onions
    7 oz (200 g) of cucumbers
    1 lb (½ kg) of tomatoes
    1 hot little pepper
    Salt, oil, parsley and grated
    cheese as needed

RECIPE:
Clean and cut 150 g (5 oz) of onions into slices, season with salt, and gently mash it for a little while. Peel 200 g (7 oz) of cucumbers and cut into thin slices. Wash ½ kg (1 lb) of tomatoes and cut them into slices too. Take one hot little pepper, and cut it into thin strips. Unite all the ingredients, then pour oil, season with salt, stir gently, sprinkle with grated fat cheese, and finish it with some chopped parsley.

SHOPSKA SALAD

INGREDIENTS:

1 lb (½ kg) of tomatoes
1 lb (½ kg) of cucumbers
7 oz (200 g) of fresh red peppers
7 oz (200 g) of fresh green peppers
2 bunches of spring onions
1 hot little pepper
Oil, salt, pepper, vinegar and grated sheep
cheese as needed

RECIPE:

Clean ½ kg (1 lb) of tomatoes, the same amount of cucumbers, 200 g (7 oz) of fresh red peppers, 200 g (7 oz) of fresh green peppers, and cut all into cubes. Put the vegetables in a bowl, add 2 bunches of spring onions cut into little rings and one hot little pepper, finely chopped. Add some oil, salt, pepper and vinegar, then stir gently, and top with grated sheep cheese.

ROASTED PEPPERS WITH GARLIC

INGREDIENTS:
10 peppers
1 head of garlic
Oil, vinegar, parsley and salt
as needed

RECIPE:
Wash 10 peppers, cook them on the stove, cover and let sit for a while. Peel and seed them. In a bowl, first place a layer of peppers, than a layer of the topping, which you prepare this way: chop a head of garlic, mix it with oil, add the cider vinegar, then season with salt and parsley. Arrange layers of peppers and topping alternately, and finish with the latter one. Sprinkle with parsley.

POTATO SALAD

INGREDIENTS:
  1,5 cup of mayonnaise
  1 tablespoon of vinegar
  1 tablespoon of mustard
  6 potatoes
  4 eggs
  Pepper and salt as needed

RECIPE:
In a deeper bowl, put a cup and a half of mayonnaise, one tablespoon of vinegar, the same amount of mustard, salt and pepper. Boil 6 potatoes in their skins, peel them and dice, then stir gently. Top these ingredients with 4 eggs, hard boiled and diced, and place the bowl in the fridge to sit for a while.

SAUERKRAUT

INGREDIENTS:
  ½ head of sauerkraut
  1 teaspoon of cayenne pepper
  Oil as needed

RECIPE:
Halve a cabbage head and cut it into strips. If it is too acidic, rinse in cold water, drain well and put into a bowl. Oil it, stir and sprinkle with cayenne pepper.

MIXED PICKLES

INGREDIENTS:
2 lb (1 kg) of carrots
2 lb (1 kg) of cucumbers
2 lb (1 kg) of peppers
2 lb (1 kg) of green tomatoes
1 lb (½ kg) of cauliflower
4.4 lb (2 kg) of cabbage
7 oz (200 g) of salt

RECIPE:
Grate 1 kg (2 lb) of large carrots, cut 1 kg (2 lb) of cucumbers into slices, cut 1 kg (2 lb) of peppers into strips, as well as 2 kg (4.4 lb) of cabbage, and chop 1 kg (2 lb) of green tomatoes and ½ kg (1 lb) of cauliflower into small pieces. Add 200 g (7 oz) of salt, stir all, fill jars and leave them covered at room temperature for 2–3 days, until they release their own juice. Close with cellophane and lids, and store in a cool place.

AYVAR

INGREDIENTS:
66 lb (30 kg) of red peppers
1.75 pt (1 l) of oil
3.5 fl oz (100 ml) of vinegar
Salt as needed

RECIPE:
Cook 30 kg (66 lb) of red peppers on the stove, arrange them in a deeper dish, cover, and let sit for some time. Peel the peppers, clean the stems and seeds, and grind. In a wide sauce-pan, pour 1 liter (1.75 pt) of oil, heat it and put in the peppers. Fry them for a long time, constantly stirring, and at the end, when ayvar has thickened (so the laddle you are stirring with leaves a noticeable trace on the bottom of the pan), pour 100 ml (3.5 fl oz) of vinegar. Add salt to taste and, while still hot, pour into heated jars, top each with a little boiled oil, and leave it overnight in the oven to brown, on the temperature of 60–80ºC (140–175 F). The cellophane and the lids with which you will close the jars, previously wipe with gauze soaked in alcohol, because it protects ayvar against spoilage.

Desserts

After a good lunch or dinner, while sipping cold wine, you should expect to be asked whether you are in a mood for something sweet. Of course you are! Serbia is a major manufacturer and exporter of fruits, but in Serbian restaurants you will not be served fresh fruits as a dessert, but only as ingredients in cakes.

Every good Serbian *kafana* (tavern, inn) aiming to live up to its reputation surely must have *suva pita sa orasima* (dry walnut pie), with a layer of rolled and lightly baked pastry, then a layer of ground walnuts, and so on. You'll see: *suva pita* is undoubtedly refreshing after a heavy meal, and with a glass of wine it's even more tasty! There is also an alternative: a cake called *orasnica* (finely chopped walnuts bound together with sugar and eggs, in the shape of a horseshoe).

If you do not like walnuts, you can choose an apple, cherry or poppy seeds strudel (flour, oil, eggs, vanilla sugar, raisins, yeast and, of course, apple, cherry or poppy seeds, respectively).

The pancakes are, by all means, something you should not miss. They are served with walnuts, jam, or chocolate, but also gratinées, or in a wine chateau. Whenever a special occasion, the pancakes are served with nuts, chocolate, butter, almonds, orange syrup, a little bit of maraschino and cognac. After being set alight before your very eyes, the pancakes are ready and served as famous flambées.

BOILED WHEAT

Ingredients:
1 lb (½ kg) of wheat
1 lb (½ kg) of ground walnuts
1 lb (½ kg) of powdered sugar
2 sachets of vanilla sugar

Recipe:
Thoroughly wash ½ kg (1 lb) of wheat, put in a pot, pour water over it, and cook at low heat for about 3 hours. During cooking, shake the pan occasionally and, if necessary, add a little hot water. When the wheat has softened, drain it, rinse and put in a strainer. Spread a table-cloth on the kitchen table, and pour the wheat on it to dry. Grind the wheat in a meat grinder, add ½ kg (1 lb) of powdered sugar, ½ kg (1 lb) of ground walnuts, 2 sachets of vanilla sugar, and knead everything well. Form into the desired shape, and sprinkle with powdered sugar.

ORASNITZE

INGREDIENTS:
- 2 lb (1 kg) of sugar
- 1.7 oz (50 ml) of water
- 5 egg whites
- 2 lb (1 kg) of walnuts

RECIPE:

Put 1 kg (2 lb) of sugar in a pan, add 50 ml (1.7 oz) of water, and cook on high heat until the sugar turns into a thick syrup. In the meantime, beat whites of 5 eggs until the stiff peaks form, add ½ kg (1 lb) of sugar, and continue beating until the sugar has melted. Slowly pour the melted sugar until the mass is homogeneous. Add ½ kg (1 lb) of ground walnuts and stir using a scoop. Take a shallow baking pan and sprinkle it with ½ kg (1 lb) of roughly ground walnuts, then put beside it a cup of water, and a spoon, which you will use to remove the walnut-sized balls from the mixture, lower in the baking pan and roll the finger-sized dumplings. Shape the orasnitze into a crescent, place them in a baking pan coated with baking paper (a little apart so they do not stick to each other) and bake with a moderate heat for half an hour.

VANILITZE

INGREDIENTS:
  7 oz (200 g) of fat or butter
  1 whole egg
  1 egg yolk
  1 lemon
  1 lb (½ kg) of flour
  1 sachet of vanilla sugar
  Powdered sugar and jam
  as needed

RECIPE:

Whisk 200 g (7 oz) of fat or homemade butter, one whole egg, one egg yolk and some lemon juice. Add ½ kg (1 lb) of flour, knead, and flatten with a rolling pin until the mixture is ½ cm (0.2 in) thick. Remove the dough with a smaller round cutter, put it into a greased pan and bake on high heat for up to 15 minutes. From this amount you will get enough material for two large baking pans, so while the first one is in the oven, you arrange the cookies in another one. Remove the first pan from the oven and, while they are hot, brush the vanilitze with jam, each from the upper side, then join them two by two, and roll in the powdered sugar mixed with one sachet of vanilla sugar.

NISH STYLE GURABIYE

INGREDIENTS:
8 oz (250 g) of fat
3 eggs
8 oz (250 g) of honey
1 lemon
1 lb (½ kg) of flour
Sugar and walnuts as needed

RECIPE:
Put 250 g (8 oz) of fat in a deeper dish and stir until fluffy, then add 2 whole eggs and one egg yolk, and continue stirring until the mixture is homogeneous. Pour 250 g (8 oz) of milk, grated rind of one lemon, stir, then add ½ kg (1 lb) of flour. Knead the dough well, flatten with a rolling pin until ½ cm (0.2 in) thick. Remove the cookies with a mold, souse them first in the beaten egg white, then in sugar and, finally, in walnuts. Arrange the cookies in coated baking pan sprinkled with flour and bake on high heat for about 10 minutes.

GINGERBREAD

INGREDIENTS:
- 2 eggs
- 8 oz (250 g) of sugar
- 2 tablespoons of honey
- 1 tablespoon of butter
- 1 teaspoon of baking soda
- ½ spoon of cinnamon
- 1 lemon
- 14 oz (400 g) of flour

RECIPE:
Whisk 2 eggs, add 250 g (8 oz) of sugar, and continue wisking until the sugar has melted. Add 2 tablespoons of honey, a tablespoon of butter, a teaspoon of baking soda, a little cinnamon, juice of one lemon and 400 g (13.5 oz) of flour. Knead the dough well and remove balls the size of walnuts, arrange them in a greased baking pan, and bake on high heat for up to 15 minutes.

SERBIAN DOUGHNUTS

INGREDIENTS:
2 lb (1 kg) of flour
1 whole egg
2 egg yolks
2 tablespoons of sugar
2 sachets of vanilla sugar
1.7 oz (50 g) of butter

RECIPE:

In a deeper plastic bowl, place 1 kg (2 lb) of flour, one whole egg and 2 egg yolks, 2 tablespoons of sugar, a pinch of salt, 2 sachets of vanilla sugar and 50 g (1.7 oz) of melted butter. Homogenize all ingredients with a mixture of milk and water. Knead the dough until it separates from the sides of the bowl. Cover it with clean cloth, and leave to swell. Knead the dough once again, adding some more flour if necessary, and then flatten it until it is 1 cm (0.4 in) thick. Remove doughnuts with a mold or a glass, and leave them on a flat surface sprinkled with flour. Let them sit for about 15 minutes, then put in hot oil. When golden brown on both sides, arrange them on paper towels which will absorb excess oil. Serve the doughnuts warm, sprinkled with powdered sugar.

LAZY PIE

INGREDIENTS:

    4 oz (125 g) of fat
    4 oz (125 g) of butter
    12 oz (350 g) of sugar
    1 sachet of vanilla sugar
    2 eggs, 1 lb (½ kg) of flour
    1 sachet of baking powder
    2 lb (1 kg) of apples
    1 teaspoon of cinnamon
    Powdered sugar and raisins as needed

RECIPE:

Whisk 125 g (4 oz) of fat with the same amount of softened butter, 150 g (5 oz) of sugar, one sachet of vanilla sugar, and add 2 eggs. Mix ½ kg (1 lb) of flour with a sachet of baking powder, add to the whisked ingredients, and knead the dough. Divide it into two equal parts, wrap each in a plastic foil, and leave in the fridge for an hour. In the meanwile, grate 1 kg (2 lb) of apples, add 200 g (7 oz) of sugar, a tablespoon of cinnamon, raisins to taste, and cook on medium heat for about 10 minutes. Spread a half of the dough in a baking pan, and flatten it with your hands. Top it with the hot apple filling, and cover it with another thin layer of dough, which you have previously flattened the same way as the first one. Bake at a moderate temperature for up to an hour. Chill the lazy pie, cut it into squares, and serve sprinkled with powdered sugar.

DRY CAKE WITH WALNUTS

INGREDIENTS:
1 lb (½ kg) of thin piecrusts
10 oz (300 g) of walnuts
1½ lb (650 g) of sugar
5 oz (150 g) of raisins
3.5 fl oz (1 dcl) of water
1 lemon

RECIPE:
For this dessert you will need ½ kg (1 lb) of thin crusts for baklava. In a bowl, mix 300 g (10 oz) of walnuts, 200 g (7 oz) of sugar, 150 g (5 oz) of raisins that you have previously soaked in water and drain. In a coated baking pan place two twin crusts sprinkled with oil, and top the mixture with walnuts. Over them place another two piecrusts sprinkled with oil, and top them as well with the walnuts, ensuring that the nuts are evenly distributed. Repeat until you have spent all the walnuts and piecrusts, and the last one anoint with a spoonful of oil. Bake the pie on medium heat for up to half an hour, and top with the syrup which you make this way: in 1 dl (3.5 oz) of water cook the 450 g (1 lb) of sugar until it gets completely liquid and takes on a dark brown colour, and then add a lemon cut into slices. Baste the baked pie with syrup, arrange lemon slices, and leave to cool.

PUMPKIN PIE

INGREDIENTS:
  3.3 lb (1,5 kg) of pumpkin
  1 lb (½ kg) of thin piecrusts
  2 sachets of vanilla sugar
  Sugar as needed

RECIPE:
Peel and grate 1,5 kg (3.3 lb) of pumpkin, and mix 2 sachets of vanilla sugar in it. From ½ kg (1 lb) of piecrusts take 2 of them, place them on the work surface, sprinkle with oil, and then put one over the other. On the longer side of the crusts build up a layer of grated pumpkin, top with 4–5 tablespoons of sugar, roll and drop into a greased baking pan. The same way you fill all crusts, arranging them one by the other in a pan. Anoint them with oil, sprinkle with water, and bake on a low heat for up to one hour. Cut the pie into pieces and sprinkle with powdered sugar.

SWEET PIE WITH CHEESE

INGREDIENTS:

4 oz (125 g) of butter
2 tablespoons of sour cream
11 oz (325 g) of sugar, 3 eggs
½ lemon, 10 oz (300 g) of flour
½ sachet of baking powder
1 lb (½ kg) of cottage cheese
1 sachet of vanilla sugar
2 tablespoons of semolina
3.5 oz (100 g) of raisins

RECIPE:

In a bowl, mix 125 g (4 oz) of butter, 2 tablespoons of sour cream, 125 g (4 oz) of sugar, one whole egg and 2 egg yolks, juice and rind of half a lemon and 300 g (10 oz) of flour mixed with half a sachet of baking powder. Knead well all the ingredients, and put dough in the fridge. In the meantime, prepare the filling: mix ½ kg (1 lb) of cottage cheese with 200 g (7 oz) of sugar, one sachet of vanilla sugar and 2 tablespoons of semolina. Whip well the egg whites and, along with 100 g (3.5 oz) of raisins, pour into the cheese. Divide the dough into two parts; take one and flatten in it a baking pan, cover it with filling, and top with another part of dough. Take the fork, stab the pie lightly in several places, and bake with moderate heat for up to one hour.

STRUDEL WITH POPPY SEEDS AND WALNUTS

INGREDIENTS:
  1 cube of yeast
  2 lb (1 kg) of flour
  5 oz (150 g) of fat
  5 oz (150 g) of sugar
  4 eggs, 1 lemon
  20 oz (600 g) of ground poppy seeds
  or walnuts, 1 pt (½ l) of milk
  14 oz (400 g) of sugar, a pinch of salt

RECIPE:

Mix a cube of yeast in lukewarm water, add a little sugar, 1 kg (2 lb) of flour, and leave to grow. In a depper bowl, mix well 150 g (5 oz) of fat, the same amount of sugar, 4 egg yolks, a little salt, grated rind of one lemon, and then add the dough. Knead all well together, cover with a clean cloth, and leave to swell. Then knead the dough again, divide it into 2 or 3 parts, and leave covered. In the meanwile, prepare the filling: 600 g (20 oz) of ground poppy seeds and/or nuts, depending on taste, boil in a pint (½ l) of milk, then add 400 g (13.4 oz) of sugar. Flatten the divided dough with a rolling pin, anoint with the filling, roll and leave to rise in a coated baking pan for up to 15 minutes more. Bake on higher heat for about an hour, cut the strudel into pieces, and sprinkle with powdered sugar.

CHERRY SOURDOUGH

INGREDIENTS:

1 pt (5 dcl) of yogurt, 1 cube of yeast
1 teaspoon of salt, 2 teaspoons of sugar
1 sachet of vanilla sugar
1 tablespoon of rum
5 oz (150 g) of butter
2 lb (1 kg) of flour, 10 oz (300 g) of sugar
5 tablespoons of cornstarch
3.5 fl oz (1 dcl) of water

RECIPE:

In a deeper dish, pour a pint (½ l) of yogurt, add a cube of yeast, a teaspoon of salt and 2 teaspoons of sugar, one sachet of vanilla sugar, a tablespoon of rum, 150 g (5 oz) of melted butter and ½ kg (1 lb) of flour, knead all well and leave the dough to proof. In another dish, put 1 kg (2 lb) of cleaned cherries with 300 g (10 oz) of sugar. Separately, mix 5 tablespoons of cornstarch with 1 dl (3.5 fl oz) of water, add the sour cream, and cook. Knead the dough again, divide it into two halves, and flatten with a rolling pin. Anoint the dough with the cherry filling, roll, and place both crusts in a greased baking pan, then brush with melted butter. Bake with higher heat for up to one hour.

NOODLES WITH POPPY SEEDS OR WALNUTS

INGREDIENTS:
1 lb (½ kg) of flour
A pinch of salt
1 tablespoon of butter
5 oz (150 g) of ground
poppy seeds or walnuts
1 sachet of vanilla sugar
½ cup of milk

RECIPE:
Put 1 kg (2 lb) of flour, a pinch of salt and some lukewarm water in a bowl, then knead the dough firmly. Flatten the dough with a rolling pin, so it is about 2 mm (0.07 in) thick, and leave to dry. Cut the crust into noodles of desired width, and drop them into boiling water for a short while. Remove the boiled noodles, strain them, wash with cold water and leave to dry completely. Lower them in warm butter, fry briefly, then remove from heat. Cook 150 g (5 oz) of poppy seeds and a sachet of vanilla sugar in half a cup of milk, until the milk has evaporated, then add sugar to taste. The same way you prepare the noodles with walnuts. Finally, add poppy seeds and/or nuts to noodles, stir, and serve.

TASHKAS WITH JAM

Ingredients:
2 lb (1 kg) of potatoes
Flour, salt, jam and bread
crumbs as needed

Recipe:
Take 1 kg (2 lb) of potatoes, cook them in their skins, then peel and mash. Add a little salt and flour, so the dough does not stick to your fingers (it should be medium soft). Flatten the dough until it is ½ cm (0.2 in) thick, and cut into little cubes. Onto each cube place a little jam, overlap two by two, and compress each end so the jam does not leak out. Place them into boiling water and, when they emerge on the surface, remove from water, put in a strainer, rinse with cold water, drop in fried bread crumbs and serve rolled in them.

PLUM DUMPLINGS

INGREDIENTS:
- 2 lb (1 kg) of potatoes
- 1 tablespoon of margarine
- 3 eggs
- 1½ lb (700 g) of flour
- 1 lb (½ kg) of plums
- Bread crumbs, sugar and cinnamon as needed

RECIPE:
Cook 1 kg (2 lb) of potatoes in their skins, peel and mash. While still warm, add one table-spoon of margarine, and stir. When the potatoes cool down, add 3 eggs and 700 g (1½ lb) of flour, and knead well. Sprinkle the work surface with flour, flatten the dough with a rolling pin until it is about 1 cm (0.4 in) thick, and cut into squares big enough that you can wrap a plum in each one of them. For this amount of flour you will need ½ kg (1 lb) of plums. When you wrap them all, place them, one by one, in salted boiling water. Cook for half an hour, until they emerge on the surface of boiling water, then drain and roll into the bread crumbs mixed with sugar and cinnamon. Allow to cool, then serve.

RASPBERRY CAKE

Ingredients:
 4 eggs
 7 oz (200 g) of sugar
 ½ sachet of baking powder
 5 oz (150 g) of flour
 2.5 oz (80 g) of butter
 300 fresh raspberries

Recipe:
Stir 4 eggs with 200 g (7 oz) of sugar until the mixture is foamy. Add 150 g (5 oz) of flour, stir all, and then add 80 g (3 oz) of melted butter. Grease a baking pan, sprinkle it with flour, pour the mixture in, top it with raspberries, and bake with a moderate heat. When baked, cut the cake into cubes, sprinkle with powdered sugar, and serve.

VASA'S CAKE

INGREDIENTS:
9 eggs, 9 tablespoons of sugar
1 tablespoon of flour
6 tablespoons of ground almonds
6 fl oz (175 ml) of milk
7 oz (200 g) of ground walnuts
3.5 oz (100 g) of chocolate
5 oz (150 g) of butter
8.5 oz (250 g) of sugar

RECIPE:

Put 5 egg yolks in a bowl, add 5 tablespoons of sugar, and beat thoroughly. Then add one tablespoon of flour and 6 tablespoons of ground almonds. Stir in 5 firmly beaten egg whites, spoon by spoon. Pour the mixture into a cake mold, and bake. When cooled, cover it with the first filling, which you prepare this way: in 175 ml (6 fl oz) of hot milk put 200 g (7 oz) of ground walnuts, and remove from heat. Whisk 4 egg yolks with 4 tablespoons of sugar, and cook by steaming; then add 100 g (3.5 oz) of chocolate, and stir until melted. Combine the mass of walnuts with a mass of chocolate, stir and, when cooled, add 150 g (5 oz) of butter. The cooled crust anoint with this filling. The other filling you will make following these instructions: cook a thick syrup of 250 g (½ lb) of sugar and 200 ml (7 fl oz) of water, then slowly add 4 egg whites, firmly beaten. Stir the mass while steaming, until it thickens. When cooled down, cover with the thick egg white filling. Garnish the cake with little candied fruits.

BELGRADE CAKE

INGREDIENTS:
    8 whole eggs
    10 egg yolks
    13 oz (380 g) of sugar
    7 oz (200 g) of almonds
    5 oz (155 g) of flour
    1 vanilla stick
    1 pt (½ l) of milk
    12 oz (350 g) of butter

RECIPE:

Mix 8 egg yolks with 170 g (6 oz) of sugar, add 150 g (5 oz) of boiled, peeled and minced almonds, 8 beaten egg whites, and 70 g (2.5 oz) of flour. Bake the dough in the greased cake molds. The filling you will prepare like this: 10 egg yolks stir well with 210 g (7 oz) of sugar, 85 g (3 oz) of flour and one vanilla stick. Mix all in a small dish, gradually adding one pint (½ liter) of milk. Cook the cream at a moderate heat, constantly stirring. When it becomes thick, remove from heat, wait for it to cool down, then add 350 g (12 oz) of butter. Cut the crust lengthwise, stuff the filling, and with the rest of the filling cover the cake from all sides. Sprinkle with boiled and finely sliced almonds.

Preserves, Compotes, Jams

There is a beautiful old custom in Serbia, although more and more suppressed lately: when the guests arrive, you first serve them with preserves made with seasonal fruits, and then offer them a glass of fresh water... Love, tradition and unique, cherished rituals and recipes that were, and still are, the trademarks of each family...

With preserves prepared and stored during autumn, you can always count on a rich winter meal, so skillful Serbian housewives work on them from spring to late autumn. The harmony of fresh fruit taste permits multi-purpose use, whether in a form of juice, a wide variety of wines and brandies, or as dried fruits, but also as compotes, marmelades, jams, or as an energetic fruit preserve, to take a spoonful each and every morning, for a successful start of a day.

PLUM PRESERVES WITH WALNUTS

INGREDIENTS:

8.5 oz (250 g) of lime
0.9 gal (4 l) of water
2 lb (1 kg) of plums
2 lb (1 kg) of sugar
2 sachets of vanilla sugar
1 lemon
1 sprig of rose geranium
Walnuts as needed

RECIPE:

Mix 250 g (8.5 oz) of lime in 4 liters (0.9 gal) of water, let the lime settle to the bottom and the water clear up. Pour the clear water in another vessel. In the meanwhile, peel 1 kg (2 lb) of plums and drop them in a lime water solution for an hour. Carefully remove them in a strainer, rinse them, pit them and, instead of each plum stone, insert a quarter of a walnut kernel. In a pan, pour a little water and 1 kg (2 lb) of sugar, cook thoroughly until it gets completely liquid and takes on a dark brown colour; then add the plums, and cook without stirring, but occasionally shaking the pan. Towards the end, add 2 sachets of vanilla sugar, the lemon cut into slices, and a sprig of rose geranium. Cover the vessel containing the cooked preserves with a clean tablecloth, wait until it cools down, and pour into the jars.

RASPBERRY PRESERVES

INGREDIENTS:
   2 lb (1 kg) of raspberries
   0.9 gal (4 l) of water
   8.5 oz (250 g) of lime
   3.3 lb (1½ kg) of sugar

RECIPE:
Pick 1 kg (2 lb) of firm raspberries and put them in lime water for an hour. In the meantime, cook 1½ kg (3.3 lb) of sugar. When it thickens, remove from heat and leave to cool. Add the raspberries and return to heat to cook, occasionally shaking the pan. When finished, remove foam from the top, cover the pan with a clean cloth, let it sit overnight, and then pour into jars.

QUINCE PRESERVES

INGREDIENTS:
- 2 lb (1 kg) of sugar
- 2 cups of water
- 3–4 quinces
- Walnuts as needed

RECIPE:

One kilogram (2 lb) of sugar boil in 2 cups of water. Peel 3 bigger or 4 smaller quinces, grate them roughly, and drop into the sugar syrup. Cook all together until the mass thickens enough. Cover the pan with a clean cloth, leave to cool, and pour into jars, along with chopped walnuts.

WATERMELON RIND PRESERVES

INGREDIENTS:
1 watermelon
1 vanilla stick
Sugar and lemon as needed

RECIPE:
Clean the watermelon rinds and dice it. These cut pieces you should boil in six waters at least. When finished, baste with cold water and leave for 24 hours, then strain. One weight of rind takes two weights of sugar. Put the sugar in a pot, pour water over, and cook, occasionally removing foam. When you obtain the desired thickness, drop pieces of rind into the sugar, and let it cook for 15 minutes. Towards the end, squeeze the juice from approximately one lemon per kilo (2 lb) of sugar, add one vanilla stick and remove foam from the top. After that, you may remove the pot from the heat, cover it with a clean cloth, and leave to cool. When chilled, pour the preserves into the jars.

PEAR COMPOTE

INGREDIENTS:
    2 lb (1 kg) of pears
    1 lb (1/2 kg) of sugar

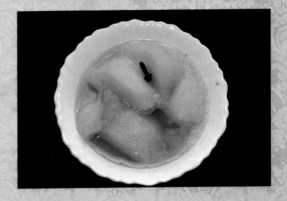

RECIPE:
Take 1 kg (2 lb) of pears, peel them, cut into halves, and clean the seeds. Place the pears in a pot, pour water until they are submerged, and cook over medium heat until soft. Arrange them in jars. In the water in which they were cooked, add ½ kg (1 lb) of sugar, boil for a short while, baste the pears with it, close the jars, and leave to cool.

QUINCE COMPOTE

INGREDIENTS:
   2 lb (1 kg) of sugar
   2 glasses of water
   3–4 quinces
   Walnuts as needed

RECIPE:
Cook one kilogram (2 lb) of sugar with a little water. Peel, quarter and seed the quinces. During the peeling, put them in boiling water, so they do not turn black, and then remove them with a slotted spoon and arrange in jars. Pour the sugar in each one, close the jars, cook by steaming for 20 minutes, then leave to cool.

ROSE HIP JAM

INGREDIENTS:
  9 lb (4 kg) of ripe rose hips
  3.3 lb (1.5 kg) of sugar

RECIPE:
Wash and stem 4 kg (9 lb) of big, ripe rose hips. Cut each one in half and clean the seeds and little hairs. Having cleaned them, wash the rose hips in three cold waters, strain, and leave covered overnight. The next day, pour the water until they are submerged, and cook, constantly stirring. When boiled, mash them, and drain through gauze to remove any hair left. Pour them back in the pot which you have washed in the meantime, add 1½ kg (3.3 lb) of sugar, return to heat and cook until the jam thickens. Pour the jam into the warm jars, then place the jars in the oven at a mild heat, to form a thin crust. Cover with cellofane first, then close with lids.

PLUM JAM

INGREDIENTS:
   9 lb (4 kg) of Hungarian plums
   2 lb (1 kg) of sugar
   1 cup of rum
   1 vanilla stick
   1 glass of vinegar
   A pinch of cinnamon

RECIPE:
Wash 4 kg (9 lb) of ripe Hungarian plums („madžarke"), and grind in the meat grinder. Pour the ground plums into a pot, and add 1 kg (2 lb) of sugar, a cup of rum, one vanilla stick, some cinnamon, and a glass of wine vinegar. Cook the jam, stirring occasionally, until the desired thickness obtained, and then, while still hot, pour into warm jars. Arrange the jars in a lightly heated oven, to form a thin crust. Cover with cellophane first, then close with lids.

CIP - Каталогизација у публикацији
Народна библиотека Србије, Београд

641.5(=163.41)(083.12)

GRBIĆ, Olivera, 1974-
  Serbian Cuisine: all the traditional
plates/Olivera Grbić; translated from
Serbian by Vladimir D. Janković. 2nd ed. – Belgrade:
Dereta, 2014 (Belgrade: Dereta). – 186 str.:
ilustr.; 19 x 21 cm

Prevod dela: Srpska kuhinja. – Tiraž 1.500.

ISBN 978-86-7346-930-0

а) Куварски рецепти, српски
COBISS.SR-ID 204253452